# THE APOLOGY HABIT RESET

A 14-day plan to stop saying sorry when you're not wrong

AMELIA OLIVER-LILLY

**THE APOLOGY HABIT RESET**



This book is provided for informational and educational purposes only. It is not intended as medical, psychological, legal, or financial advice, and it is not a substitute for professional support, diagnosis, or treatment. While the author has made reasonable efforts to ensure the accuracy of the information in this book, no guarantee is made that the content is complete, current, or suitable for every reader or situation. Readers are encouraged to seek guidance from qualified professionals regarding their individual circumstances.

Any examples, scenarios, or reflections in this book are presented for illustrative purposes. They may be generalized, anonymized, or composite in nature. Any resemblance to actual persons, living or dead, is coincidental.

The author and publisher shall not be liable for any loss of profit or any other damages, including but not limited to special, incidental, consequential or other damages, arising directly or indirectly from the use or misuse of the information contained in this book.

First edition

Paperback and eBook

Cover and interior design by Big Fat Web

Published by Upload Makers Publishing

# Contents

# INTRODUCTION
# THE APOLOGY HABIT RESET

If "sorry" is one of your most used words, you probably don't need anyone to point it out. You already hear it in your own voice. You see it in your texts. You feel it arrive the moment there is a pause, a delay, or a hint of tension.

This book isn't about becoming tougher, colder, or "more assertive." It's about becoming more accurate.

Some apologies repair trust. Others are a reflex, a social safety move that tries to prevent discomfort. When "sorry" becomes your default, it can quietly teach you to take responsibility for things that are not yours: other people's moods, other people's disappointment, other people's opinions. Over time, that has a cost. You feel smaller. You explain too much. You hesitate to ask for what you need. You agree to things you resent. You replay conversations that other people have already forgotten.

*The Apology Habit Reset* is a practical guide for replacing automatic apologies with calm, clear language that keeps warmth without self-blame. You'll learn how to tell the difference between a real repair apology and an anxiety apology. You'll learn what to say instead when you're not at fault. And you'll practice the skills in small, real-life reps that don't require you to change your personality.

**What this book will do**

- Help you notice your apology patterns without shaming you
- Show you simple replacement moves you can use immediately
- Give you scripts that sound normal, not robotic
- Help you hold boundaries without apology padding
- Help you apologize well when you are actually wrong
- Give you a short reset plan you can follow without making your life complicated

**What this book won't do**

- It won't tell you to stop apologizing altogether
- It won't push you into confrontations for the sake of "confidence building"
- It won't diagnose you or try to treat mental health issues
- It won't promise guaranteed outcomes
- It won't make your goal "winning" conversations or controlling other people's reactions

**A better goal than "stop saying sorry"**

A lot of advice about over-apologizing is built around a rigid idea: never apologize, speak like a boss, don't care what anyone thinks. If that approach worked for you, you would have done it already.

**A more useful goal is accuracy.**

Accurate apologies are specific, calm, and paired with repair. Inaccurate apologies often show up when you're uncomfortable, not when you're wrong.

Accuracy keeps your kindness and restores your self-respect.

**Two questions that change the habit**

Throughout this book, you'll return to two short questions. They matter because they create a pause between trigger and reflex.

1. Am I actually at fault?

2. What am I trying to prevent?

The first question protects real accountability. The second question reveals the job your apology is doing. When you can name the job, you can choose a better tool.

**The simple model you will practice**

You don't need a hundred new phrases. You need a small set of moves that match common situations. This book gives you that set.

You'll learn how to:

- spot the moments where "sorry" is acting as filler or comfort
- map your trigger types so you can predict your hot spots
- speak with one sentence first so you stop over-explaining
- choose a replacement move instead of apology padding
- repair cleanly when you make a real mistake
- set boundaries without turning them into negotiations
- handle pushback with calm repetition and exits when needed

None of these skills require you to be loud. They require you to be clear.

**How to use this book**

This book is designed for real life. You can read it straight through, or you can jump to the chapters that match your main problem.

If you want the fastest change, do two things as you read:

- Pick one small rep each day and try it in a low-stakes moment.
- Write one receipt sentence afterward. A receipt is a short note that proves you practiced.

Examples of receipts:

- "I replaced sorry with thanks for timing once."
- "I asked a question without apology padding."
- "I held a boundary without adding new reasons."

Receipts matter because your brain trusts evidence more than motivation.

**A note about relationships and reactions**

As you change your language, some people will barely notice. Others will notice right away. Someone may joke that you sound "direct." Someone may push back. Someone may test the boundary.

This is normal.

Your job isn't to manage every reaction. Your job is to keep your communication clean and respectful. If you do that, you can let your message stand.

**The practice mindset**

You're not trying to pass a test. You're training a habit.

Some days you will do a clean rep and feel calm. Other days you will do a clean rep and feel awkward. Both count.

*The plan is simple:*
small reps, repeated often enough to become available when you're tired, stressed, or unsure.

If you're ready, start with Chapter 1. You'll learn how to sort "sorry" into the types that repair versus the types that shrink you, and you'll take a one-day snapshot that shows your real patterns.

**A quick reminder before you start**

If you've used apology as a safety move for years, change can feel surprisingly personal. Keep your first goal small.

One rep is enough. One clean sentence is enough. One boundary held without a story is enough.

Your job isn't to fix every relationship at once. Your job is to practice clarity in the moments that matter most to you.

# CHAPTER 1
# THE HIDDEN COST OF AUTOMATIC SORRY

If you say "sorry" a lot, you probably already know it.

You notice it in texts. You hear it when you ask a question. You feel it show up the second there's a pause, a delay, or even a hint of tension. Sometimes it slips out so quickly you only realize afterward, when your stomach drops and you wonder why you apologized at all.

This book isn't here to take kindness away from you. It's here to help you stop paying for kindness with self-blame.

You can be considerate without shrinking. You can be warm without acting at fault. You can apologize when it matters, and stop apologizing when it doesn't.

This chapter explains what automatic apologies cost you over time, even when they seem harmless in the moment. It also gives you a simple way to start noticing what kind of "sorry" you're using, so changing the habit later feels practical instead of overwhelming.

**Start here**

- Over-apologizing is often a habit you learned, not a flaw you are.
- Many apologies are used to prevent discomfort, not repair harm.
- Automatic sorry can blur your message and weaken boundaries.
- You can keep warmth and remove self-blame at the same time.
- Today you'll learn the apology spectrum and do a one-day snapshot.

**What's really going on**

A real apology has a job. It repairs. It acknowledges impact. It shows accountability. It helps rebuild trust.

But when "sorry" becomes your default, it often stops doing that job. It turns into a social safety move, something you use to smooth a moment before it has a chance to get uncomfortable.

That's why over-apologizing can be confusing. On the surface it looks polite. It can even sound thoughtful. People might call you "easygoing" or "nice" and mean it as a compliment.

And yet the habit can quietly create problems in your relationships and inside your own head.

**The hidden costs of automatic sorry**

**Cost 1:** It shifts the focus from your message to your guilt.

When you lead with "sorry," the other person hears an emotional signal first. Your actual point comes second. That matters when your message is a request, a clarification, a boundary, or even a simple update. The content can get buried under cushioning.

**Cost 2:** It teaches people that your needs are negotiable.

Apology language often carries uncertainty. Even when you don't mean it that way, it can sound like you're asking permission to have a need or a limit. Some people won't take advantage of that, but the pattern still changes the conversation. It invites more back-and-forth than you intended.

**Cost 3:** It increases your mental load.

Over-apologizing rarely comes alone. It's often followed by extra explaining, extra reassurance, and a follow-up message "just in case." Then comes the replay: Did I upset them? Did I sound rude? Should I send another message? You spend energy managing reactions that may not even exist.

**Cost 4:** It creates resentment.

If you apologize to keep the peace but it costs you honesty, you can start feeling invisible. You might keep being agreeable. You might keep smoothing. But something in you keeps track of how often you swallow what you actually wanted to say.

**Cost 5:** It weakens true repair.

If "sorry" is everywhere, it becomes background noise. When you genuinely make a mistake, your apology has less contrast. It can land less strongly, not because you don't mean it, but because you've used the same word for everything from being late to asking a question.

This book will help you protect the power of real apologies by using them accurately, and by using other tools when you're not at fault.

### Courtesy, repair, and self-blame

A useful shift is learning to separate three things that often get tangled together.

**Courtesy**
Respectful language that acknowledges someone's time, space, or effort. Courtesy is normal and healthy.

**Repair**
A real apology for real wrongdoing or real impact. Repair matters, and it stays in this book.

**Self-blame**
Apologizing for existing, for having needs, for taking time, for asking, for being human. Self-blame is optional, and it's the part we're removing.

Courtesy and repair support relationships. Self-blame drains them.

## The apology spectrum

Instead of thinking "apology or no apology," it helps to think in a spectrum. Most "sorry" moments fall into one of these buckets.

### 1) Filler sorry

This is "sorry" used as punctuation. It doesn't mean you did anything wrong. It's often automatic.

Examples:

- *"Sorry, quick question."*
- *"Sorry to bother you."*
- *"Sorry, just checking."*

### 2) Comfort sorry

This "sorry" tries to soothe a moment. You might be trying to prevent someone being annoyed, disappointed, or uncomfortable.

Examples:

- *"Sorry, I know you're busy."*
- *"Sorry, I'm probably being annoying."*
- *"Sorry, I don't want to be a pain."*

**3) Courtesy sorry**

This is where "sorry" can be polite without being self-blame. Some people prefer "excuse me" or a neutral line instead, but courtesy sorry isn't automatically wrong.

Examples:

- *"Sorry, can I squeeze past?"*
- *"Sorry, I didn't realize you were on a call."*

**4) Clarity sorry**

This "sorry" appears when you correct or clarify. Often it can be replaced with a clean clarification.

Examples:

- *"Sorry, I meant Thursday."*
- *"Sorry, what I meant was..."*

**5) Repair sorry**

This is the apology you keep. It's for real wrongdoing or real impact.

Examples:

- *"I'm sorry I forgot. I can see that affected you."*
- *"I'm sorry I spoke sharply. That wasn't okay."*

In this book, the focus is reducing filler and comfort sorry. We'll also strengthen clarity, requests, boundaries, and repair so you're never left wondering what to say instead.

**Why your brain reaches for sorry**

Most over-apologizers aren't trying to be dramatic. They're trying to reduce social risk.

If you learned that tension is dangerous, or that disapproval is expensive, you may have developed a quick solution: apologize early, soften the moment, lower the chance of conflict.

That solution can work short-term. It can keep things calm. It can protect you from uncomfortable reactions. It can keep you feeling "safe" in the interaction.

But it also teaches your brain that self-blame is the price of smoothness.

The work in this book is replacing that price with better tools.

**Accountability vs appeasement**

One reason over-apologizing sticks is that it can feel like responsibility. You're owning the moment. You're showing you care. You're trying to be considerate.

But there's a difference between accountability and appeasement.

***Accountability*** is when you take responsibility for what is actually yours. You name what you did, you name the impact, and you make it right when you can.

***Appeasement*** is when you take responsibility for other people's comfort, other people's moods, or other people's disappointment, even when you didn't cause harm.

Appeasement often sounds like:

- *"Sorry I asked."*
- *"Sorry I'm taking up your time."*
- *"Sorry I'm like this."*
- *"Sorry, I know I'm being annoying."*

Those lines don't repair anything. They try to lower the chance of rejection.

If you've been using appeasement for a long time, you may feel a quick sense of relief when the other person responds kindly. That relief is real, and it's part of why the habit repeats.

The goal of this book isn't to remove your care. It's to remove the idea that care requires self-blame.

**The three-question check**

When you feel "sorry" rising, you can run a quick check that takes about five seconds.

1. **Did I cause harm or break an agreement?**
If yes, repair may be appropriate.

2. **Am I trying to prevent a reaction?**
If yes, you're probably in comfort sorry territory.

3. **What would be kinder and clearer than sorry right now?**
Often, it's appreciation, clarity, a request, or a boundary. This is the same two-question frame from the introduction, plus a third question that turns awareness into a usable next line.

This check is especially useful if you tend to apologize for things that are normal: needing time, needing space, changing your mind, asking for clarification, or saying no.

### A note about "sorry" as a habit word

Some people use "sorry" the way they use "like" or "um." It's a filler word, not a moral statement.

If that's you, you don't need to police every "sorry." You're not trying to sound perfect.

What you're looking for is the "sorry" that carries weight, the one that makes you feel smaller. The one that turns your message into a plea. The one that pulls you into over-explaining.

Those are the moments this book is designed to change.

A simple clue is what happens right after you say it.

If you say "sorry" and then you:

- add a long explanation
- offer extra reassurance
- backtrack from what you meant
- feel anxious and want to send another message

That's usually not courtesy. That's the habit doing its old job.

**Where automatic sorry shows up most**

If you're not sure whether this is "a thing" for you, look for these common situations. They're not dramatic. They're ordinary, which is why the habit can be hard to notice.

- **Late replies:** you apologize for not replying fast enough, even when no deadline existed.

- **Questions:** you apologize before asking, as if curiosity needs permission.

- **Preferences:** you apologize for liking what you like, or for wanting something different.

- **Corrections:** you apologize before you clarify, even when you're simply being accurate.

- **No's:** you apologize while setting a limit, then soften it until it disappears.

- **Silence:** you apologize to fill space, especially if you sense the other person's impatience.

Try a quick experiment today: in one of these situations, remove the apology and keep the warmth.

- Instead of *"Sorry for the late reply,"* try *"Thanks for your patience."*
- Instead of *"Sorry, quick question,"* try *"Quick question."*
- Instead of *"Sorry, I can't,"* try *"I can't, but thanks for thinking of me."*

You're not being rude. You're being clear, and clear is easier for other people to respond to.

**What success looks like this week**

A lot of people quit early because they expect the habit to vanish. That's not realistic, and it's not required.

For the next seven days, define success like this:

- You notice one apology moment you used to miss.
- You swap one "sorry" for a clearer tool.
- You let the message stand without sending a second apology.

That's enough.

Small wins matter here because they build evidence. Evidence is what makes your brain trust that you can be clear and still be safe.

**Easy mistakes to watch for**

**Trap 1**: Turning this into a self-improvement crusade.

You're not trying to become a different person. You're updating a habit.

**Trap 2**: Making "never apologize" the goal.

Not the goal. You'll still apologize when it's appropriate. You'll just stop apologizing when you're not at fault.

**Trap 3**: Replacing sorry with bluntness.

Clarity does not require harshness. There are warm ways to be direct.

**Trap 4**: Over-analyzing every apology.

This is a practical book. The goal isn't perfect awareness. The goal is a few better choices each week.

**Trap 5**: Using your habit as proof you're "too much."

The habit likely helped you at some point. You don't need to attack it. You just need to update it.

**How to do this**

This chapter's skill is learning to spot the difference between apology that repairs and apology that cushions discomfort.

Here's a simple five-step method you can use immediately.

**Step 1: Notice the moment**

When you feel the urge to say "sorry," pause for one beat. You don't need a long pause. Just enough to notice.

If you need a neutral phrase while you pause, try:

- *"One moment."*
- *"Give me a second."*

**Step 2: Ask the accuracy question**

Ask yourself:

- "Am I actually at fault?"

Fault means you did something wrong or caused harm you're responsible for.

Fault does not mean:

- someone is disappointed
- a plan changed
- you needed time
- you asked a question
- you had a preference

If the answer is yes, you may need repair. If the answer is no, you need a different tool.

**Step 3: Identify the bucket**

Pick the closest bucket:

- filler
- comfort
- courtesy
- clarity
- repair

You're not trying to be perfect. You're building a new kind of awareness: quick and useful.

**Step 4: Name your intention**

What do you actually need to do right now?

Common intentions include:

- share an update
- ask a question
- make a request
- clarify a detail
- set a boundary
- apologize for real harm

Naming the intention helps you stop treating "sorry" as the entry fee for speaking.

**Step 5: Use one clean sentence**

Say one clear sentence that matches your intention.

Examples:

- **Update**: *"I'm running 15 minutes late."*
- **Question**: *"Can you clarify what time we're meeting?"*
- **Request**: *"Could you send me the address?"*
- **Boundary**: *"I can't make it tonight."*
- **Repair**: *"I'm sorry I forgot. I can see how that affected you."*

You'll build more options later. For now, the win is noticing the moment and choosing accuracy over reflex.

**What this looks like in real life**

Here are two everyday scenarios that show the difference between reflex apology and accurate communication.

**Scenario 1: You need more time**

Someone texts: *"Can you let me know today?"*

You feel the pressure. Your brain wants to smooth the moment.

You're about to type: *"Sorry, I'm so slow. I'm sorry. I just need more time."*

Run the steps:

- Notice the moment: you feel urgency.
- Accuracy question: are you at fault for needing time? No.
- Bucket: comfort sorry, trying to prevent disappointment.
- Intention: set a timing boundary.
- One clean sentence: *"I need more time. I can let you know by tomorrow afternoon."*

Optional warmth without self-blame:
*"Thanks for your patience."*

Final message: *"I need more time. I can let you know by tomorrow afternoon. Thanks for your patience."*

If they push, you don't need to collapse into apology mode. You can repeat the timing boundary:

*"I understand you'd like an answer today. I can't give you a good one today. I'll let you know tomorrow afternoon."*

**Scenario 2: You say no to a plan**

A friend invites you to something you don't want to do. You're tired, you need a quiet night, and you don't have the capacity.

Your reflex might be:
*"I'm so sorry, I feel terrible. I wish I could. I'm sorry."*

Run the steps:

- Notice the moment: guilt rises.
- Accuracy question: are you at fault for needing rest? No.
- Bucket: comfort sorry, trying to prevent disappointment.
- Intention: set a boundary.
- One clean sentence: *"I can't make it tonight."*

Optional warmth without self-blame:
*"Thanks for thinking of me, and I hope it goes well."*

Final message: *"I can't make it tonight. Thanks for thinking of me, and I hope it goes well."*

That's a boundary with warmth, without self-blame.

**Scripts you can use**

These scripts are designed for Chapter 1 only. They're starter options for replacing reflex apologies without getting too far ahead of the book.

**Micro script set 1:** Replace filler and comfort sorry

1. *"Quick question."*
2. *"Can I check something?"*
3. *"I need a minute to think."*
4. *"Thanks for your patience."*
5. *"I appreciate you waiting."*
6. *"Here's the update."*
7. *"To clarify..."*
8. *"That won't work for me."*

**Micro script set 2:** Warmth without self-blame

1. *"Thanks for understanding."*
2. *"I appreciate it."*
3. *"I get that this is inconvenient."*
4. *"I hear you."*
5. *"Thanks for being flexible."*
6. *"I care about this."*
7. *"I want to be clear."*
8. *"I'm not able to do that."*

**A quick practice**
**Practice: Swap one "sorry" today**

1. Choose one situation where you often apologize automatically.
2. Decide what you actually need to do: update, request, clarify, boundary, or repair.
3. Say it in one sentence without "sorry."
4. If you want warmth, add one appreciation line, not self-blame.
5. Stop there and let it be enough.

A good first swap is changing *"Sorry for the late reply"* to *"Thanks for your patience."*

**Try this**
**The 24-Hour Sorry Snapshot**

This exercise gives you data without turning the day into a self-judgment project.

**Step 1: Track your apologies for 24 hours**

Tally every time you say or type:

- sorry
- my bad
- I'm so sorry
- sorry to bother you
- sorry, quick question

Don't try to stop yourself. Just track.

**Step 2: Add a five-word label**

Next to each tally, write what happened in five words or less.

Examples:

- "late reply"
- "asked a question"
- "needed more time"
- "said no"
- "clarified a detail"

### Step 3: Sort each one into a bucket

Label each apology as:

- filler
- comfort
- courtesy
- clarity
- repair

### Step 4: Circle the comfort and filler ones

These are usually where the fastest change lives.

### Step 5: For two circled items, answer three prompts

Write a short answer to each:

1) What was I trying to prevent?
2) Was I actually at fault?
3) What would a clean alternative be: appreciation, clarity, request, or boundary?

### Step 6: Choose one replacement line

Pick one circled item and choose one line to use next time.

Examples:

- *"Thanks for your patience."*
- *"To clarify..."*
- *"I need more time."*
- *"That won't work for me."*

**Step 7: Define success**

Write one sentence:
*"Success this week is using my replacement once."*

If tracking for a full day feels like too much, do a half-day snapshot. The pattern will still show up.

**If this feels hard**
**"If I don't apologize, I feel rude."**

That feeling is common. It often comes from equating politeness with self-blame. Try a small experiment: replace "sorry" with appreciation in a low-stakes moment.

Instead of *"Sorry I'm late,"* try: *"Thanks for waiting."*
Most people experience that as polite, not rude.

**"But I did inconvenience them."**

Sometimes you did. Inconvenience doesn't always equal wrongdoing, but you can still acknowledge it without self-attack.

Try: *"I know that was inconvenient. Thanks for your patience."*

**"I'm afraid they'll think I'm selfish."**

This is a common fear for people who've been praised for being easy. If you communicate clearly and respectfully, you're not being selfish. You're being accurate.

Also, you're not required to manage every reaction in advance. That's part of the habit you're changing.

**"I catch myself apologizing mid-sentence."**

That's normal. If you notice it, you can correct gently without making it a big deal.

Try: *"Let me rephrase that."* Then say the clean sentence.

**"What if I'm actually wrong?"**

Then you apologize well, and you stop. A real apology is covered later in the book. For now, focus on reducing apologies that are driven by discomfort rather than fault.

**Take this with you**

- Many automatic apologies are used to prevent discomfort, not repair wrongdoing.
- The apology spectrum helps you sort "sorry" into filler, comfort, courtesy, clarity, and repair.
- The accuracy question keeps you from taking blame when you're not at fault.
- Warmth can come from appreciation and respect, not self-blame.
- A one-day snapshot gives you a clear starting point without overthinking.

**Coming up**

Next, you'll map your personal apology triggers and identify what job "sorry" is doing for you in the moments it shows up fastest.

# CHAPTER 2
# YOUR APOLOGY TRIGGERS AND THE JOB "SORRY" IS DOING

You don't apologize at the same rate all day.

Most people who over-apologize have hot spots. The same kinds of moments keep pulling the word out of you fast: a short reply, a plan change, a request, a hint of disappointment, or a question you think you should already know the answer to.

This chapter helps you find your hot spots and name what your apologies are trying to do for you in those moments.

Once you can name the job, you can choose a better tool without having to fight yourself.

**Start here**

- Triggers are predictable situations that spike your urge to smooth and apologize.
- A reflex apology is often trying to prevent a reaction, not repair harm.
- Your body usually signals the trigger before you speak.
- When you know the trigger type, you can choose a starter line that fits the moment.
- By the end of this chapter, you'll have a Trigger Map and two practice reps.

**What's really going on**

A trigger isn't proof that you did something wrong.

A trigger is a moment where your system expects social risk. You might expect annoyance, disappointment, judgment, tension, being misunderstood, or being rejected. The reflex apology shows up as a quick attempt to reduce that risk.

Instead of asking, "Why am I like this?" ask something more useful:

- What is my apology trying to prevent right now?

- When you can answer that, you stop treating the reflex as a mystery. You also stop blaming yourself for it. You're not weak. You're patterned.

## The jobs "sorry" is doing

Most reflex apologies are trying to do one of these jobs:

- Prevent disappointment: keep someone from feeling let down by you.
- Prevent anger: keep the moment from escalating.
- Prevent judgment: avoid looking rude, careless, foolish, or incompetent.
- Prevent rejection: avoid being seen as a burden or "too much."
- Prevent misunderstanding: protect your intent from being read harshly.
- Prevent tension: smooth the vibe, fill the silence, keep things light.

None of these jobs are evil. They're protective. The problem is that "sorry" is a blunt tool. It often adds self-blame where none is needed, and it can invite more apologizing and explaining than the moment requires.

## The six trigger types

Your triggers usually fall into a small set of types. You don't need to fix all of them. You need to identify your top two, then practice replacement moves in low-stakes moments.

1. **Time triggers**
Delays, late replies, running behind, needing more time, rescheduling.

2. **Request triggers**
Asking for help, stating a need, making a request, expressing a preference.

3. **Disagreement triggers**
Correcting a detail, expressing a different view, saying no, setting limits.

4. **Uncertainty triggers**
Not knowing, asking a question, needing clarification, deciding.

5. **Mood triggers**
Someone sounds irritated, cold, impatient, disappointed, or "off."

6. **Evaluation triggers**
You feel assessed or judged, even in everyday settings like family dynamics, social groups, or service interactions.

**Why naming the trigger changes everything**

If you don't know your trigger, you rely on your old safety move.

If you do know your trigger, you can plan a new first line.

That first line is what keeps you from apologizing and then spiraling into explanations. You don't need a perfect conversation. You need a stable first move.

**Easy mistakes to watch for**

- Treating triggers as flaws. They're patterns, not identities.
- Mapping everything. Start with your top two.
- Trying to eliminate discomfort. The goal is tolerance, not total comfort.
- Using one person's reaction as your scoreboard. Track your choices, not their mood.
- Over-correcting into coldness. You can be warm without self-blame.

**How to do this**

This is the simplest way to work with triggers in real time.

**Step 1: Catch the pre-sorry signal**

There's usually a tiny moment before the apology. The signal might be a thought like:

- "They're going to be annoyed."
- "I'm bothering them."
- "I need to soften this."
- "This could turn into conflict."
- "I'm about to look stupid."
- "I need to fix the vibe."

You don't need to argue with the thought.
You just need to catch it.

**Step 2: Ask the prevention question**

Ask yourself:
*What am I trying to prevent right now?*

Answer with one word if possible: disappointment, anger, judgment, rejection, tension, misunderstanding.

**Step 3: Notice your body cue**

Your body often reacts first. Common cues:

- you start speaking faster
- your breath gets shallow
- your throat tightens
- you smile automatically
- you rush to fill silence
- you type a long message, then add more
- you feel a stomach drop

Pick one cue you notice most. That becomes your early warning signal.

**Step 4: Label the trigger type**

Time, request, disagreement, uncertainty, mood, or evaluation.

This isn't labeling you. It's labeling the moment so you can choose the right tool.

**Step 5: Choose the replacement goal**

Instead of apologizing, choose what you actually need to do:

- Pause: buy time so you don't default to sorry.
- Gather info: ask a neutral question instead of assuming.
- Clarity: state the message cleanly.
- Appreciation: acknowledge patience or flexibility.
- Request: ask directly.
- Boundary: set a limit.

**Step 6: Use a starter line and stop**

A starter line is your first stable sentence.

Say it, then pause. Don't add a paragraph to justify it. If the other person needs more, they can ask.

**What this looks like in real life**

**Scenario 1: Request trigger with hidden guilt**

A friend texts: *"Can you come over tonight and help me set this up?"*

Your body cue hits. You feel pressure to be easy. You imagine them being disappointed.

Your fingers want to type: *"Sorry, I don't think I can, I'm so sorry, I've just got a lot on."*

Map it.

**Pre-sorry signal:** "They'll think I don't care."
**Prevention goal:** prevent disappointment and judgment.
**Trigger type:** request.
**Replacement goal:** boundary, with warmth if you want.

A clean response: *"I can't tonight. I hope it goes smoothly."*

If you want to offer an alternative, only do it if it's real: *"I can't tonight. I can help for 30 minutes tomorrow."*

If they push, you don't need to earn your no: *"I still can't tonight."*

Notice what changed. The boundary is clear. Warmth is present. Self-blame is gone.

**Scenario 2: Mood trigger that leads to mind reading**

You send: *"Can you confirm what time we're meeting?"*
They reply with one word: *"Later."*

Your brain interprets tone and tries to fix it. You want to say: *"Sorry, I didn't mean to bother you."*

But you don't actually know what's happening. This is where mood triggers get you into trouble. You apologize for a story you invented. Use a gather-info starter line: *"Is now a good time, or should I check back tonight?"*

If they say, *"Busy,"* you reply: *"Got it. I'll check back tonight."*
If they say, *"Stressed,"* you reply: *"No problem. We can sort it later."*

You stayed respectful. You didn't take blame for their mood.

## Scripts you can use

These script sets are unique to Chapter 2 and won't be reused later.

### Micro script set 1: Trigger interrupt prompts

1) What am I trying to prevent right now?
2) Is this fault or discomfort?
3) What is the simplest truthful sentence?
4) Do I need a pause before I answer?
5) Am I about to over-explain?
6) What information do I actually need?
7) What boundary or request is hiding here?
8) Can I let this be normal?

### Micro script set 2: Starter lines by trigger type

1) Time: "Thanks for your patience. I'll update you later."
2) Request: "I can help with one part, not the whole thing."
3) Disagreement: "I don't see it that way."
4) Uncertainty: "I'm not sure yet. I'll check."
5) Mood: "Is this a good time to talk?"
6) Evaluation: "Give me a second to think."
7) Boundary: "That won't work for me."
8) Clarity: "Let me be clear about what I mean."

**A quick practice**
**Practice: One trigger, one starter line**

Pick one trigger you know you have today. When it shows up, do three things:

1) Name the trigger type in your head.
2) Ask what you're trying to prevent.
3) Use one starter line from the 'Scripts you can use'.

Then stop. Let the moment unfold. Your job is the first move, not controlling the whole interaction.

**Try this**
**The Trigger Map**

This exercise turns your patterns into a plan you can use this week.

**Step 1: List five reflex-apology moments**
Write five moments where you tend to apologize quickly, especially when you're not at fault.

**Step 2: Write the prevention guess**
For each moment, finish: "If I don't apologize, they might..."

**Step 3: Name the label your brain attaches**
Finish: "And that would mean I'm..."

**Step 4: Identify the trigger type**
Time, request, disagreement, uncertainty, mood, or evaluation.

**Step 5: Choose the replacement goal**
Pause, gather info, clarity, appreciation, request, or boundary.

**Step 6: Write one starter line**

One sentence you can use immediately.

**Step 7: Choose your top two triggers**

Circle the two that show up most.

**Step 8: Build a two-rep plan**

Write:

- When ____ happens, I will ____.
- My starter line is ____.

**Step 9: Define success**

Success this week is using your starter line once for each trigger.

That's two reps total.

**A section that makes the plan stick**

Identifying triggers is useful, but the habit often wins after you speak. You send a clear message, then you panic and soften it with an extra apology or a long explanation.

This section gives you three upgrades that make your new responses more available in real life.

**Upgrade 1: Spot trigger stacking**

Sometimes it's not one trigger. It's two.
Common stacks:

- time plus evaluation: you're late and you feel watched
- request plus mood: you ask and the other person sounds cold
- disagreement plus rejection: you say no and fear they'll pull away
- uncertainty plus judgment: you don't know and fear looking foolish

When triggers stack, your brain rushes harder. It wants to smooth faster. Use a pause starter line: "I need a second to answer clearly."

Then choose your goal: clarity, appreciation, request, boundary, or gather info.

**Upgrade 2: The ten-minute rule for follow-ups**

A lot of over-apologizing happens after the first message, not before it.

Try this for the next week:

If your message was clear and respectful, don't send a second message for ten minutes.

If you still want to explain after ten minutes, write the explanation in your notes first. Then decide if it actually helps.

Most of the time, it doesn't.

**Upgrade 3: One sentence of context, not a defense speech**

Sometimes a small amount of context is helpful. The issue is when context becomes a defense speech.

Use this guideline:
One sentence of context is enough.

Example: *"I can't tonight. I have a full evening."*

Then stop. No extra paragraphs. No guilt performance.

If someone needs details, they can ask. You don't need to pre-explain to earn your boundary.

**If you want to go a bit further: Build your personal trigger card**

If you want this to feel easier in the moment, make a small trigger card you can keep in your phone notes. It takes three minutes, and it gives your brain a shortcut when the reflex hits.

1. Write your top two trigger types. Example: time and mood.
2. For each trigger, write the prevention job in one phrase. Example: prevent disappointment.
3. Choose one body cue that tells you it's happening. Example: rushing to reply.
4. Pick one starter line you will use first for each trigger.
5. Choose one repeat line for pressure. Example: *"That still doesn't work for me."*
6. Add one calm exit line for circular conversations. Example: *"I'm going to pause this and come back later."*

**If this feels hard**
**"I can't tell what I'm trying to prevent."**

Try:

- What feels risky right now?
- What reaction would bother me most?
- What am I trying to keep smooth?
- What do I assume they'll think of me?

Even "tension" is a useful answer.

**"My triggers are mostly about one person."**

If one person reliably pulls you into apology mode, start with a pause starter line.

*"I need time to think."*
*"I'll get back to you."*

**"I noticed the trigger but still apologized."**

That's normal. The win is noticing. Next time, aim for one breath before you respond.

**"What if they really are judging me?"**

They might be. You can't control that. You can control whether you apologize for having normal needs.

**Take this with you**

- Triggers are predictable moments that spike your urge to apologize and smooth.
- The prevention question reveals the job your apology is trying to do.
- Body cues help you catch the trigger earlier than your words.
- Starter lines give you a stable first move that replaces reflex sorry.
- Two low-stakes reps per week is enough to start changing the pattern.

**Why your triggers feel so urgent**

Triggers don't just show up in your thoughts. They show up as urgency. Urgency sounds like:

- "Fix this right now."
- "Say something before it gets awkward."
- "Make sure they're not mad."
- "Explain so they don't misunderstand."

Urgency isn't proof you're wrong. It's your system trying to reduce uncertainty.

A helpful mindset shift is this:

You don't need to remove urgency to respond well. You need a plan that works even when urgency is present.

That's why we're building starter lines. A starter line gives you something to do while the urgency is still there.

**The trigger loop in plain language**

Most reflex apologizing follows the same loop:

1) A trigger hits.
2) Your brain predicts a reaction.
3) Your body signals threat.
4) You apologize to prevent the reaction.
5) You feel brief relief.
6) The relief teaches your brain to do it again next time.

This loop isn't your fault. It's how habit learning works.

Your job is to break the loop at step 4. You don't break it by telling yourself to "be confident." You break it by choosing a different first move.

**Three common trigger profiles**

You might recognize yourself in one of these. These are not labels. They're patterns.

**Profile 1: The smoother**

Your main fear is tension. You apologize to keep interactions light. You might say sorry when:

- there's silence
- someone's tone shifts
- you need to correct something small
- you want to exit a conversation

Your replacement focus is pause plus clarity. Your starter lines should buy time and reduce mind reading.

**Profile 2: The burden-avoider**

Your main fear is being too much. You apologize for needing anything.

You might say sorry when:

- you ask for help
- you state a preference
- you take up time
- you want reassurance

Your replacement focus is direct requests and clean appreciation. Your starter lines should normalize needs without self-blame.

**Profile 3: The mistake-preventer**

Your main fear is judgment. You apologize to avoid looking wrong.

You might say sorry when:

- you don't know something
- you ask a question
- you need clarification
- you correct yourself mid-sentence

Your replacement focus is uncertainty tolerance and clear questions. Your starter lines should protect your dignity while you gather info.

You can have elements of more than one profile. That's normal.

**What this looks like in real life**

**Scenario 3: Uncertainty trigger without self-blame**

You're making plans with someone and they say: *"Just pick a place. You decide."*

Your brain might interpret this as pressure. What if you choose wrong. What if they judge you?

Your reflex might be: *"Sorry, I'm terrible at picking. Sorry, I don't know."*

Map it:

- **Prevention goal:** prevent judgment.
- **Trigger type:** uncertainty plus evaluation.
- **Replacement goal:** pause plus request for input.

A clean response: *"I can choose. Before I do, what matters most to you, quiet or lively?"*

If they say *"either,"* you can choose with a clear offer: *"Okay. I'll pick a quiet place. If you'd prefer lively, tell me now."*

This is not indecisive. It's collaborative without apology padding.

**Scripts you can use add-on: Texting templates**

These lines help when your trigger hits during texting and you feel the urge to over-explain.

*1) "Quick check: are we still on for 6?"*
*2) "I can reply tonight. Thanks for your patience."*
*3) "I can't do that. I hope it works out."*
*4) "To clarify, I meant Thursday, not Tuesday."*
*5) "I'm not sure. I'll confirm and get back to you."*
*6) "Is now a good time, or should we talk later?"*
*7) "I need more time. I'll decide by tomorrow afternoon."*
*8) "I'm going to pause this and come back to it."*

**Try this**
**The 48-hour trigger diary**

This is a short diary, not a deep emotional project. You're collecting patterns.

**Step 1: Choose a window**
Pick the next two days. Any two days.

**Step 2: Track only the hot spot moments**
You're not tracking every apology. You're tracking the moments that felt urgent.

When you feel the urge to apologize quickly, write a quick note.

**Step 3: Use this simple format**

Write one line for each moment:

- Trigger type:
- Prevention goal:
- Body cue:
- What I said:
- What I wish I'd said:

Example:

- Trigger type: *mood*
- Prevention goal: *prevent tension*
- Body cue: *rushed typing*
- What I said: *"Sorry, I didn't mean to bother you."*
- What I wish I'd said: *"Is now a good time, or should I check back later?"*

**Step 4: Circle your top two trigger types**

At the end of day two, look for repeats. Circle the two trigger types that showed up most.

**Step 5: Choose one starter line per trigger**

For each of the two trigger types, pick one starter line. Keep them short.

**Step 6: Set a two-rep plan**

For each trigger, plan one low-stakes rep this week. Write: *"When ____ happens, I will use ____."*

**Step 7: Define success**

Success is doing the rep, not feeling calm.

This diary works because it ties your starter lines to real moments, not imagined ones.

**Take this with you**

- Triggers create urgency, but urgency isn't proof you're at fault.
- The trigger loop repeats because apologies create short-term relief.
- Naming your trigger type helps you choose a replacement goal fast.
- Starter lines work best when they match your personal trigger profile.
- A short trigger diary gives you real data and a simple practice plan.

**Coming up**

Next, you'll learn the Clean Communication Rule, which gives you a simple structure for being clear without sounding cold.

# Chapter 3
# The Clean Communication Rule

If you've been over-apologizing for a long time, you may have learned a quiet rule: To be kind, I have to soften myself.

That rule shows up in small ways. You add extra words. You add extra reassurance. You add an apology before you even know if you did anything wrong. You explain in advance so nobody can misunderstand you.

Chapters 1 and 2 helped you spot the pattern and the triggers. This chapter gives you the missing piece: a simple rule you can use in the moment to keep your communication clear, respectful, and steady.

Not tougher. Not colder. Clearer.

**Start here**

- Clean communication separates clarity from self-blame.
- One sentence first is often enough to stop over-explaining.
- Warmth is optional and can come from appreciation, not apology.
- You can be direct without being harsh.
- Today you'll practice a rewrite method you can use in texts and conversations.

**What's really going on**

In Chapter 1 you learned that many "sorry" moments are about preventing discomfort rather than repairing harm. In Chapter 2 you mapped the triggers that pull that reflex out of you.

Now you need a rule that works in any trigger moment, whether you're texting, speaking, or deciding what to say.

*Here it is:*

Clarity is required.
Warmth is optional.
Self-blame isn't required.

This rule does three things at once.

1) It makes clarity the standard, not perfection.

2) It keeps you connected without requiring you to shrink.

3) It removes the idea that you have to apologize to be acceptable.

**What clean communication is**

Clean communication is language that is:

- clear about the message
- respectful in tone
- free of unnecessary self-blame
- short enough to be understood quickly
- steady enough to stand without a follow-up apology

It's not robotic. It's not "always assertive." It's simply accurate.

**What clean communication is not**

It's not:

- a performance of confidence
- a blunt personality shift
- a lecture
- a long defense speech
- a promise to keep everyone happy

Clean communication does not guarantee that someone will like what you say. It does guarantee that what you say is easier to understand and respond to.

**Why "one sentence first" matters**

When you're triggered, your brain wants to manage risk. It tries to prevent misunderstanding, conflict, or disappointment by adding more words. More words feel safer.

The problem is that more words often create more openings for confusion and negotiation.

One sentence first forces your message to have a shape. It makes your point visible. Then, if context is actually useful, you can add it after.

Think of it like this:

- **Sentence 1** is the message.
- **Sentence 2** is optional warmth or the next step.

Then stop.

You're not trying to sound perfect. You're trying to stop building a case for your right to speak.

**Easy mistakes to watch for**

- Confusing clean communication with harsh communication.
- Using warmth as an excuse to add self-blame back in.
- Adding context to control the other person's reaction.
- Over-editing your words because you want a guaranteed good outcome.
- Turning a simple message into a full explanation because you feel exposed.

You'll still be thoughtful.
You'll just be thoughtful without apologizing for existing.

### How to do this

Here's a practical method you can use in almost any situation.

### Step 1: Choose the message type

Most situations fit one of these types:

- **Update:** share what's happening.
- **Request:** ask for something.
- **Boundary:** say no or set a limit.
- **Clarify:** correct or restate.
- **Pause:** buy time to respond.

Repair is handled later in the book. For this chapter, the goal is clear communication when you're not at fault.

### Step 2: Write the one sentence first

Say the core message in one sentence.

Examples:

- **Update:** *"I'm running 15 minutes late."*
- **Request:** *"Can you send me the address?"*
- **Boundary:** *"I can't do tonight."*
- **Clarify:** *"To clarify, I meant Thursday."*
- **Pause:** *"I need a minute to think."*

If you can't make it one sentence, you're likely mixing messages. Decide what matters most and lead with that.

**Step 3: Remove self-blame language**

Self-blame isn't the same as politeness.

Remove or avoid phrases like:

- *"Sorry to bother you"*
- *"This is probably stupid"*
- *"I'm being annoying"*
- *"I'm the worst"*
- *"I hate to ask"*

If you feel the urge to include one of these, that's a trigger signal. Use a pause line instead.

**Step 4: Add optional warmth that doesn't weaken the message**

Warmth can be one line.

Good warmth lines:

- *"Thanks for your patience."*
- *"I appreciate it."*
- *"Thanks for understanding."*
- *"I know this is inconvenient."*

Avoid warmth that turns into self-attack:

- *"I feel terrible."*
- *"I'm so sorry you have to deal with me."*

**Step 5: Add context only if it helps**

Context is useful when it:

- prevents practical confusion
- provides a next step
- answers a likely question

Context isn't useful when it:

- begs for approval
- tries to control someone's reaction
- turns your message into a defense

A simple guideline: One sentence of context is enough.

**Step 6: Send and stop**

Over-apologizers often undo a clean message by sending a second message. If your first message was clear and respectful, let it stand.

If you want a guardrail: No follow-up for ten minutes.

**What this looks like in real life**

**Scenario 1: Clean requests without apology padding**

You want to ask someone a simple question.

Your reflex is to soften: *"Sorry, quick question, I know you're busy, but could you maybe send the link when you get a chance, sorry."*

Clean communication version: *"Can you send me the link today? Thanks."*

If you want more warmth: *"Can you send me the link today? I'd appreciate it."*

Notice what you removed:

- permission seeking
- self-blame
- the extra apologies

You kept respect. You kept clarity. You made it easier for the other person to answer.

If they can't do it today, they can say: *"I can do tomorrow."*

Now you have useful information.

**Scenario 2: Clarifying without shrinking**

Someone repeats a detail incorrectly.

Your reflex is to apologize before correcting: *"Sorry, I might be wrong, but I think it's actually at 6."*

Clean communication version: *"To clarify, it's at 6."*

If you want to add warmth: *"To clarify, it's at 6. Thanks for checking."*

Clean communication isn't about winning. It's about making your meaning visible without turning the correction into a guilt performance.

**Scripts you can use**

These script sets are unique to Chapter 3 and focus on clean phrasing and stopping over-explaining.

**Micro script set 1: One sentence first templates**

1) "Here's the update: ____."
2) "My answer is ____."
3) "I need ____."
4) "I can't ____."
5) "I can do ____ instead."
6) "To clarify, ____."
7) "My request is ____."
8) "I need time. I'll reply by ____."

**Micro script set 2: Warmth lines that don't add self-blame**

1) *"Thanks for your patience."*
2) *"I appreciate it."*
3) *"Thanks for understanding."*
4) *"Thanks for checking."*
5) *"I know this is inconvenient."*
6) *"I'm glad you asked."*
7) *"I hear you."*
8) *"I want to keep this clear."*

**A quick practice**
**Practice: One sentence, then stop**

Pick one message you need to send today. Before you send it:

1) Write one sentence first.
2) Add one warmth line if you want.
3) Send it.
4) Do not add a follow-up for ten minutes.

This is a small practice, but it's a powerful one. It teaches your brain that clarity can stand on its own.

**Try this**
**The No Extras Drill**

This drill teaches you to separate your message from your defense.

**Step 1: Choose three recent messages**

Pick texts or emails where you apologized, over-explained, or added too much reassurance.

**Step 2: Rewrite each using the clean structure**

- Sentence 1: message (update, request, boundary, clarify, or pause)
- Sentence 2: optional warmth or next step

**Step 3: Circle what you removed**

Common extras include:

- repeated apologies
- disclaimers (“this is dumb”)
- long reasons that don’t change the outcome
- reassurance begging (“please don’t be mad”)

**Step 4: Read your rewrite out loud**

Ask:

- Is it clear?
- Is it respectful?
- Did I remove self-blame?

**Step 5: Use one rewrite this week**

Pick the one that feels slightly uncomfortable but still doable.

That’s your practice rep.

**If this feels hard**
**“I feel rude when I’m brief.”**

Brief isn’t rude. Lack of respect is rude.

If you’re clear and respectful, brevity is usually a kindness. It saves time and reduces confusion.

If you want warmth, add one line of appreciation. That often resolves the “I sound harsh” fear without bringing apology back in.

**"I'm worried they'll misunderstand me."**

This is a common trigger. Use a clean clarify line: *"To clarify, I mean ____."*

Then stop. If they still misunderstand, you can clarify again. You don't need to pre-clarify with three paragraphs.

**"I sent the clean message and now I want to add more."**

That urge is the old habit trying to buy safety.

*Use this rule:* If your message was clear and respectful, don't add more for ten minutes.

If it still feels urgent after ten minutes, add one sentence of context, not a full defense.

**"Some situations really do need more detail."**

Yes. Clean communication doesn't ban detail. It changes the order.

Lead with the message. Add only the detail that helps the person respond.

**If your trigger is silence**

Silence can feel like danger when you're used to smoothing. You may rush to fill the space with an apology or extra explaining.

Try a different move:

- Take one slow breath.
- Let the silence stay for two seconds.
- Then use a clean sentence.

Examples:

"Here's what I can do."
"I need more time to think."
"That doesn't work for me."

Silence isn't automatically disapproval. Sometimes it's just processing.

**A quick reset for over-explaining**

If you notice you're adding more and more detail, pause and use this reset:

1) Write your message as one sentence.
2) Ask: "Does this sentence stand on its own?"
3) If yes, send it.
4) If no, add only one sentence of context.

That's it. Two sentences max.

Over-explaining often looks like politeness, but it can read like uncertainty. Clear and brief is usually kinder for both of you.

## If you want to go a bit further: Clean communication in three common formats

Clean communication can feel different depending on where you're speaking. Here's how to apply the same rule in three formats without drifting into over-explaining.

### Format 1: Text messages

Text is where apology padding grows fast because you can keep editing and adding. Use this structure:

- line 1: the message
- line 2: optional warmth or next step

Examples:

- *"I can't make it tonight. Thanks for understanding."*
- *"I need more time. I'll reply by tomorrow afternoon."*
- *"Can you send the address? I'd appreciate it."*

If you catch yourself writing a third line, ask: *Is this helping them respond, or am I trying to prevent a feeling?*

### Format 2: In person conversations

In person, the trigger is often silence. You may rush to fill space with apologies or extra reasons. Try this:

- say the one sentence
- pause
- let the other person react

Example: *"I can't do Saturday."*

Pause.

If you want to keep warmth: *"I can't do Saturday. I hope it goes well."*

Pause.

**Format 3: When you feel pressured**

Pressure makes you talk more. If you feel rushed, use a pause line first:

*"Give me a second. I want to answer clearly."*

Then deliver your one sentence. Pressure isn't an emergency. You're allowed to slow down.

**If you want to go a bit further: The clarity swap list**

Here are common apology-heavy phrases and clean swaps. Use one this week.

- *"Sorry to bother you" > "Quick question."*
- *"Sorry I'm late" > "Thanks for waiting."*
- *"Sorry, I'm confused" > "Can you clarify ____?"*
- *"Sorry, I can't" > "I can't."*
- *"Sorry, I need to reschedule" > "I need to reschedule. Can we do ____?"*
- *"Sorry, I forgot" > "I missed that. Here's what I'm doing now."*

These are not magic lines. They are reminders that you can be polite without putting yourself at fault.

### If you want to go a bit further: The two-sentence boundary

If you struggle with boundaries because you start explaining, use this template for a week.

**Sentence 1:** the boundary.
**Sentence 2:** optional warmth or alternative.

Examples:

- *"That won't work for me. Thanks for understanding."*
- *"I can't do that today. I can do it tomorrow afternoon."*
- *"I'm not available. I hope it goes well."*

If you need to repeat, repeat the first sentence only.

### The clean communication mindset shift

Clean communication becomes easier when you separate three things that often get tangled together.

### 1) Being clear is not being intense

Some people avoid clarity because they associate it with confrontation. But clarity is simply a clear message delivered in a normal tone.

Intensity is a different thing. Intensity shows up as:

- raised voice
- sarcasm
- rushed speech
- blaming
- dramatic language

You can be clear without any of that.

**2) You don't need to "earn" a normal request**

Many over-apologizers feel like requests require permission. They add extra softeners so the other person won't judge them.

But normal requests are part of normal relationships. The other person can say yes or no. You don't need to pre-shrink to make your request acceptable.

**3) You can care about a reaction without taking responsibility for it**

You can acknowledge that something is inconvenient or disappointing without turning it into self-blame.

Acknowledgment sounds like:

- "I get that this is inconvenient."
- "I can see you were hoping for a different answer."

Self-blame sounds like:

- "I'm terrible."
- "I feel awful for being like this."

The first keeps connection.
The second puts you underneath.

**What to do when you're tempted to over-explain**

Over-explaining usually comes from one of these fears:

- I won't be believed.
- I'll be judged.
- They'll be mad.
- They'll misunderstand me.
- They'll think I don't care.

If you notice that fear, try this sequence:

1) Name the fear privately: "This is the judgment fear."
2) Restate your one sentence message.
3) Add one helpful detail only if it changes logistics.
4) Stop.

This works because it keeps the message stable, even if your feelings are not.

**What this looks like in real life**

**Scenario 3: Setting a boundary without a story**

Someone asks you to do something you don't want to do. You say yes out of discomfort, then regret it.

A common apology-heavy no looks like: *"Sorry, I can't, I've just been really overwhelmed, and I feel bad, and I wish I could."*

Clean version: *"I can't do that."*

If you want warmth: *"I can't do that. Thanks for understanding."*

If you want an alternative that is real: *"I can't do that. I can do a shorter version on Thursday."*

The difference isn't attitude. The difference is that you're not putting your boundary on trial.

**Scenario 4: Asking for clarification without shrinking**

You don't understand something and you feel exposed.

Your reflex is to apologize: *"Sorry, I'm confused. Sorry, this might be dumb."*

Clean version: *"Can you clarify what you mean by ____?"*

If you want warmth: *"Can you clarify what you mean by ____? I want to get it right."*

You didn't apologize for not knowing. You used a normal question.

**Scripts you can use add-on: Clean "pause" lines**

Use these when you feel rushed or pressured to answer. They protect you from blurting out apologies or extra explanations.

1) *"Give me a second to think."*
2) *"I want to answer clearly. One moment."*
3) *"I'm not ready to respond yet."*
4) *"Let me check and get back to you."*
5) *"I need a minute."*
6) *"I'm going to think about that and reply later."*
7) *"I'm not sure. I'll confirm."*
8) *"I'm going to be clear, then we can talk about details."*

### If you want to go a bit further: The rewrite ladder

When you're learning clean communication, it helps to rewrite the same message in stages. This keeps you from jumping from "soft" to "too blunt" in one move. Start with what you would normally say, then make these edits.

**Stage 1: Remove apology padding**

Delete apologies that are not repair. Delete *"sorry to bother you," "sorry this is dumb,"* and similar softeners.

**Stage 2: Remove permission language**

Delete *"just," "maybe," "possibly," "if that's okay,"* when you're making a normal request or stating a normal boundary.

**Stage 3: Make the message one sentence**

Force yourself to name the main point in one sentence. If you need a second sentence, make it warmth or next step.

**Stage 4: Add a helpful detail only**

Add one detail that helps the other person respond. Avoid details that are there to make you look better.

**Stage 5: Stop**

This is the hardest stage. Don't keep editing to feel safe.

Here's a quick example.

Original: *"Sorry to bother you, I know you're busy, but could you maybe send the form when you get a chance. Sorry."*

Clean: *"Can you send the form today? Thanks."*

Notice how the clean version gives the other person something concrete to answer.

**A second exercise: The one-sentence workout**

If you want fast progress, do this for three days in a row.

1) Choose one message you need to send today.
2) Write the one sentence first.
3) Add one warmth line or a timeline.
4) Send it.
5) Write one receipt: "I sent a clear message and let it stand."

The point is not to feel calm. The point is to practice clarity while you feel a little exposed.

**If this feels hard add-on: When someone says "Why are you being so direct"**

If someone notices the change, you don't need a speech. Try one of these:

- *"I'm trying to be clearer."*
- *"I want to say what I mean."*
- *"I'm practicing simpler communication."*
- *"I don't want to over-explain."*

That's enough. You don't need to defend clarity.

**If you want to go a bit further: A small script menu for common moments**

**Late reply:**
*"Thanks for your patience. Here's the update."*

**Reschedule:**
*"I need to reschedule. Can we do ____ instead."*

**Need time:**
*"I need more time. I'll reply by ____."*

**Say no:**
*"That won't work for me."*

**Clarify:**
*"To clarify, I mean ____."*

These are normal sentences. Using them isn't rude. It's clean.

**If you want to go a bit further: Clean communication when emotions are present**

Clean communication is not only for neutral moments. It also helps when you feel annoyed, hurt, or overwhelmed.

The goal is not to hide emotion. The goal is to express it without blame and without a flood of explanation.

Use this three-part template:

1) Name the feeling in one word.
2) Name the issue in one sentence.
3) Name the next step.

Examples:

- *"I'm frustrated. I need us to agree on a time. Can we decide by tonight?"*
- *"I'm overwhelmed. I can't take on more right now. I'll revisit it next week."*
- *"I'm disappointed. I want to talk it through. Can we talk tomorrow?"*

This keeps you honest without turning the moment into a long justification.

If you notice yourself drifting into explanations, return to the next step sentence. Next steps calm the conversation.

**A final scenario: When you need to correct yourself**

Sometimes you send an apology-heavy message and you want to clean it up. You do not have to send a big follow-up. Keep it simple.

Instead of: *"Sorry, I didn't mean that, I'm so sorry, I feel terrible."*

Try: *"Let me restate that clearly: ____."*

Then stop.

This teaches your brain that you can correct without performing guilt.

### Quick check before you hit send

Before you send a message, ask:

- Is my first sentence clear?
- Did I remove self-blame?
- Did I add only helpful detail?
- Can I let this stand?

If yes, send it and stop.

### Take this with you

- Clean communication rule: clarity is required, warmth is optional, self-blame is not required.
- One sentence first makes your meaning visible and reduces over-explaining.
- Warmth can come from appreciation and respect, not apology padding.
- Context should help the other person respond, not control their reaction.
- Let a clear message stand before adding more.

### Coming up

Next, you'll learn the Replacement Ladder, a simple set of moves that shows you exactly what to say instead of "sorry" in common real-life situations.

# Chapter 4
# The Replacement Ladder: What to Say Instead

In the moments you usually apologize, you don't need a better personality. You need a better option.

Most reflex apologies happen fast. You feel a jolt, you sense risk, and "sorry" arrives before you've even chosen what you want to say. Then the apology pulls extra words behind it, because you're trying to make sure the other person stays comfortable.

Chapters 1 to 3 helped you spot the habit, map the triggers, and communicate cleanly. This chapter gives you a tool you can use under pressure: a simple ladder of replacements. You won't have to invent the "right" sentence on the spot. You'll choose the right move.

**Start here**

- Most unnecessary apologies can be replaced with a small set of moves.
- The Replacement Ladder helps you choose the correct move quickly.
- Appreciation, clarity, requests, and boundaries often work better than "sorry."
- You can keep warmth without adding self-blame.
- Today you'll build a personal ladder menu you can use this week.

**What's really going on**

The ladder answers one question:
*If I'm not at fault, what do I say instead of "sorry"?*

Earlier, you learned to ask whether you're actually at fault and to keep your first sentence clear. Now you need the next piece: a map of alternatives that fit real situations.

The Replacement Ladder has five moves. Each one matches a common trigger moment.

1) Remove filler
2) Appreciation
3) Clarity
4) Request
5) Boundary

The point isn't to sound clever.
The point is to be accurate.

When you replace an unnecessary apology with the correct move, three things happen:

- your message becomes easier to respond to
- you stop putting yourself underneath
- you reduce the urge to over-explain afterward

**How to choose the right ladder move**

Use this quick decision path.

**Step 1: Am I actually at fault?**

If yes, that is repair. Repair gets its own chapter next.
If no, continue.

**Step 2: What is the main job of my message?**

- I'm opening a message and "sorry" is just filler > remove filler
- I'm dealing with timing or waiting > appreciation
- I'm correcting or restating > clarity
- I'm asking for something > request
- I'm saying no or limiting access > boundary

If you're unsure, choose clarity. Clarity is usually safer than apology padding.

**Easy mistakes to watch for**

- Using appreciation when you really need a boundary.
- Using clarity to debate instead of clarify.
- Turning requests into long stories so they feel "acceptable."
- Adding apology padding after you've already made the ladder move.
- Overusing the same move for everything because it feels safest.

The ladder works best when you match the move to the situation.

**How to do this**

**Step 1: Pause for one breath**

You don't need a dramatic pause. One breath is enough to interrupt the reflex.

If you need a line to buy time: *"Give me a second. I want to answer clearly."*

**Step 2: Decide whether repair is needed**

Ask: Am I actually at fault?
If yes, you'll use the repair structure in the next chapter.
If no, you pick a ladder move.

**Step 3: Pick the ladder move**

Choose one of the five moves. Then say one sentence first.

**Step 4: Add optional warmth**

Warmth can be appreciation, acknowledgement, or a simple respectful tone. Do not add self-blame.

**Step 5: Stop**

The ladder works when you let your message stand. If you keep talking to feel safe, you'll slide back into apology mode.

**Ladder move 1: Remove filler**

This is for when "sorry" is basically punctuation.

Common filler openers:

- *"Sorry, quick question."*
- *"Sorry to bother you."*
- *"Sorry, just checking."*

Most of the time, you can delete "sorry" and keep the message.

Instead of: *"Sorry, quick question. Are we still on for 6?"*
Try: *"Quick question. Are we still on for 6?"*

If you want warmth: *"Quick question. Are we still on for 6? Thanks."*

Remove filler is the smallest move, but it changes your baseline fast.

**Ladder move 2: Appreciation**

Appreciation replaces apology for timing issues and waiting.

Instead of: *"Sorry for the late reply."*
Try: *"Thanks for your patience."*

Instead of: *"Sorry I'm running behind."*
Try: *"Thanks for waiting. I'll be there at 6:15."*

Appreciation is respectful without putting you at fault for being human.

**Ladder move 3: Clarity**

Clarity replaces apology when you need to correct, clarify, or restate.

Instead of: *"Sorry, I might be wrong, but I think it's actually Thursday."*
Try: *"To clarify, it's Thursday."*

If you want warmth: *"To clarify, it's Thursday. Thanks for checking."*

Clarity is not aggression. It's a clean restatement.

**Ladder move 4: Request**

Requests replace apology when you're asking for something: help, time, a decision, information, a change.

Instead of: *"Sorry to bother you, but could you maybe send the info."*
Try: *"Can you send the info today?"*

Optional warmth: *"Can you send the info today? I'd appreciate it."*

The goal is normal requests in normal language.

**Ladder move 5: Boundary**

Boundaries replace apology when you're saying no, limiting something, or protecting your time and energy.

Instead of: *"Sorry, I can't. I feel terrible."*
Try: *"I can't."*

If you want warmth: *"I can't. Thanks for understanding."*

If you want an alternative that is real: *"I can't tonight. I can do tomorrow afternoon."*

Boundaries are information, not a debate.

**What this looks like in real life**

**Scenario 1: Rescheduling without apology padding**

You need to reschedule plans. Your reflex is to apologize a lot and explain why.

Old pattern: *"I'm so sorry, something came up, I feel terrible, can we reschedule, I'm sorry."*

Use the ladder.

Am I at fault?
No. Life changed.

Main job
It's a timing change. That's appreciation plus request.

Clean version: *"I need to reschedule. Can we do Thursday instead? Thanks for being flexible."*

If they respond with disappointment: *"I get it. I know it's annoying. Thursday is what I can do."*

You stayed warm and clear without turning the reschedule into a guilt performance.

**Scenario 2: Saying no to a favor with a real limit**

Someone asks: *"Can you help me with this today?"*

Your reflex is to apologize and then explain every reason you can't.

Use the ladder.

Am I at fault?
No.

Main job
Boundary, possibly with an alternative if you want.

Clean version: *"I can't today."*

Optional warmth: *"I hope it goes smoothly."*

If you can offer something real: *"I can't today. I can help for 20 minutes tomorrow."*

If they push: *"I still can't today."*

The boundary stays short. The repeat stays calm.

**Scripts you can use**

These script sets are unique to Chapter 4 and focus on ladder moves in real situations.

**Micro script set 1: Ladder move openers**

1) Remove filler: *"Quick question."*
2) Appreciation: *"Thanks for your patience."*
3) Appreciation: *"Thanks for waiting."*
4) Clarity: *"To clarify, ____."*
5) Clarity: *"Let me restate that."*
6) Request: *"Can you ____ today?"*
7) Boundary: *"That won't work for me."*
8) Boundary: *"I can't do that."*

### Micro script set 2: Short follow-ups that don't undo the move

1) *"Here's what I can do: ____."*
2) *"My answer is still no."*
3) *"I can do ____ instead."*
4) *"I'll reply by ____."*
5) *"Thanks for understanding."*
6) *"I hear you."*
7) *"I can see that's frustrating."*
8) *"Let's decide by ____."*

### A quick practice

### Practice: One ladder move today

Pick one ladder move to practice today. Then choose one real moment where you can use it.

Examples:

- remove filler in one text message
- use appreciation instead of apologizing for timing
- use clarity to correct one detail
- make one request without apology padding
- set one small boundary without a story

After you do it, write one receipt:
"I used ____ instead of sorry."

**Try this**
**The Ladder Pick Drill**

This is the exercise that turns your common "sorry" moments into ready replacements.

**Step 1: List five moments where you apologize unnecessarily**
Use simple labels like: late reply, reschedule, ask for help, clarify, say no.

**Step 2: Choose the ladder move for each**
Remove filler, appreciation, clarity, request, or boundary.

**Step 3: Write one sentence first for each moment**
Keep it short.

**Step 4: Write one optional second sentence**
Warmth or next step only. No self-blame.

**Step 5: Choose your top three scripts**
These become your "this week" set.

**Step 6: Practice them out loud once**
Slowly. Calmly. One time each.

**Step 7: Use one script this week**
Success is using it once, not feeling confident.

**If this feels hard**
**"Appreciation feels fake."**

Keep it simple. *"Thanks for waiting."* If you don't want warmth, use a clear update instead.

**"Requests feel demanding."**

A normal request is not a demand. Keep your tone calm. You can add "I'd appreciate it" if you want, but skip apology padding.

**"Boundaries make me feel selfish."**

A boundary is information. If you can't, you can't. Short and calm is often kinder than yes with resentment.

**"I keep adding explanations."**

That's the habit trying to buy safety. Use the two-sentence limit: message, then warmth or next step. Then stop.

**If you want to go a bit further: The 10-second ladder choice**

If you want the ladder to work under stress, you need a fast way to choose a move.

Ask yourself these three questions:

1) **What is the person actually waiting for?**
Information, a yes or no, a correction, or an update.

2) **What would make it easiest for them to respond?**
A clear sentence that names the point.

3) **Which ladder move matches that?**

- Information or update > appreciation or remove filler
- Correction > clarity
- Asking > request
- Saying no > boundary

Then deliver one sentence. If your brain wants to explain, that is a sign you chose the right move and your habit is resisting it.

**Scenario 3: Clarity without debate**

Someone insists on a detail that you know is incorrect. You're tempted to soften into vagueness.

Ladder move: clarity.

Try: *"To clarify, the time is 6."*

Pause.

If they argue: *"I hear you. I'm still going with 6."*

This keeps the moment from turning into a long justification.

**Scenario 4: Appreciation without over-promising**

You're late responding and you want to smooth it by promising you'll do better forever.

Ladder move: appreciation plus clarity.

Try: *"Thanks for your patience. I can confirm ____."*

Avoid adding a promise you can't keep. Clear and present is enough.

**If you want to go a bit further: A mini menu for your top triggers**

Pick your top three trigger moments and pre-write your ladder lines. Keep them in your notes.

1) **Late reply**: *"Thanks for your patience. Here's the update."*

2) **Reschedule**: *"I need to reschedule. Can we do ___ instead."*

3) **Saying no**: *"That won't work for me."*

If you want a fourth:

4) **Clarify**: *"To clarify, I mean _____."*

Pre-writing removes pressure. You're not rehearsing to sound perfect. You're reducing the chance you'll apologize out of panic.

**A second exercise option: The before-and-after rewrite set**

If writing five scripts feels too abstract, use this instead.

1) Write three sentences you often use that include apology padding.

Examples: *"Sorry to bother you..." "Sorry, I can't..." "Sorry, quick question..."*

2) For each, write a ladder replacement in one sentence first. Remove filler, appreciation, clarity, request, or boundary.

3) Add one optional warmth line that does not include self-blame.

*"Thanks for understanding." "I appreciate it."*

4) Send one replacement this week and do not send a follow-up apology.

This is a faster way to get real practice with less planning.

**Quick check before you send**

Before you hit send, ask:

- Did I choose a ladder move?
- Is my first sentence clear?
- Did I avoid self-blame?
- Can I let this stand?

If yes, send it and stop.

**When the ladder feels "too direct"**

A common fear is that removing apologies will make you sound blunt. Often, what feels "too direct" is simply unfamiliar.

Here is a quick way to soften without self-blame.

You keep the ladder move and add one of these, only one:

- **appreciation**: *"Thanks for your patience."*
- **acknowledgement**: *"I know this is inconvenient."*
- **connection**: *"I care about this."*
- **next step**: *"Here's what I can do."*

You do not add:

- repeated apologies
- self-attack
- long reasons meant to prove you're a good person

**Softening examples by ladder move**

Remove filler: *"Quick question. Are we still on for 6."*
Softened: *"Quick question. Are we still on for 6. Thanks."*

Appreciation: *"Thanks for waiting. I'll be there at 6:15."*
Softened: *"Thanks for waiting. I'll be there at 6:15. I appreciate your flexibility."*

Clarity: *"To clarify, it's Thursday."*
Softened: *"To clarify, it's Thursday. Thanks for checking."*

Request: *"Can you send the link today?"*
Softened: *"Can you send the link today? I'd appreciate it."*

Boundary: *"I can't do tonight."*
Softened: *"I can't do tonight. I hope it goes well."*

The move stays intact. Warmth is added without turning into guilt.

**Ladder mistakes that keep you stuck**

If the ladder isn't working, it's usually because of one of these mistakes.

1) **You choose the correct move, then you undo it.**

Example: *"I can't tonight."*
Undo: *"I'm so sorry, I feel terrible, and I just have so much going on."*

2) **You choose appreciation when you need a boundary.**

Example: *"Thanks for understanding"* when the person is still pushing for a yes.

In that case, switch to: *"That won't work for me."*

3) **You choose clarity and then you debate.**

Clarity is a restatement, not an argument. Say it once, then stop.

4) **You choose a request and then you beg.**

A request can include warmth, but it should not include self-blame.

5) **You choose a boundary and then you negotiate yourself down.**

If you offer an alternative, make it real and specific. If you don't want to offer an alternative, don't.

**A second set of scenarios you can practice this week**

**Scenario 3: Asking for help without apology padding**

You need help with something small. Your reflex is to apologize for the ask.

Old: *"Sorry to bother you, but could you maybe help me with this if you're not too busy."*

Ladder move: request.

Clean: *"Can you help me with this today?"*
If you want warmth: *"Can you help me with this today? I'd appreciate it."*

If they say no, you don't apologize for asking. You say: *"Got it. Thanks anyway."*

That response keeps your dignity intact and keeps the relationship normal.

**Scenario 4: Ending a conversation without apology**

You're in a conversation that's going in circles. Your reflex is to apologize and keep talking.

Ladder move: boundary.

Clean: *"I'm going to pause this for now."*
Optional warmth: *"I want to talk about it, just not like this."*

You're not shutting the person down forever. You're ending a loop.

### Exercise add-on: Your ladder rules for the next seven days

Write these rules at the top of a note. They are meant to be simple and enforceable.

- I will not apologize for asking a normal question.
- I will use appreciation for timing instead of sorry.
- I will clarify once, then stop.
- I will ask directly, then stop.
- I will say no without a story.

Pick two rules to focus on this week. Success is one rep per rule.

### Build your "ladder kit" for the situations you face most

The ladder becomes reliable when you stop using it only in emergencies. Build a small kit for your most common situations.

### Kit category 1: Timing and updates

Write one line for each:

- **Late reply:** *"Thanks for your patience. Here's the update: ____."*
- **Running late:** *"Thanks for waiting. I'll be there at ____."*
- **Need more time:** *"I need more time. I'll reply by ____."*

These are not apologies. They are clear updates with respect built in.

**Kit category 2: Requests and small asks**

Write one line for each:

- **Ask for info**: *"Can you send me ____ by ____?"*
- **Ask for help**: *"Can you help me with ____?"*
- **Ask to change plans**: *"Can we shift ____ to ____?"*

If you want warmth, add it as a second sentence: *"I'd appreciate it."*

**Kit category 3: Boundaries and no's**

Write one line for each:

- **Simple no**: *"That won't work for me."*
- **Decline a request**: *"I can't do that."*
- **Protect time**: *"I'm not available today."*

If you want a relationship-friendly ending: *"Thanks for understanding."*

**Kit category 4: Clarifications**

Write one line for each:

- **Correct detail**: *"To clarify, ____."*
- **Restate intent**: *"Let me restate what I mean: ____."*
- **Confirm agreement**: *"Just to confirm, we're doing ____."*

Once you have these written, you don't have to invent language under stress.

**How to practice without making your life complicated**

You don't need to practice with your hardest person first. You practice with low-stakes reps.

Try this three-day loop and repeat it:

**Day 1**: remove filler once
**Day 2**: use appreciation once
**Day 3**: set one small boundary

That's it. Three reps, not thirty.

Each rep teaches your nervous system the same lesson: you can be clear without apologizing.

**A final scenario: The "clarify then request" combo**

Sometimes your reflex apology is hiding two messages: you need to clarify, and you need to ask for a change.

Example: *"Sorry, I think I might have misunderstood, sorry, can we maybe do Friday instead."*

Ladder move: Clarity first, then request.

Clean: *"To clarify, I can't do Thursday. Can we do Friday instead?"*

Optional warmth: *"Thanks for being flexible."*

This is a common combination, and it becomes much easier once you see it as two clean moves rather than one long apology.

**Quick reminders for the moments you freeze**

Some people don't over-apologize because they talk too much. They over-apologize because they freeze and then try to recover by smoothing.

If you freeze, use one of these ladder-safe lines to restart:

- "Let me be clear about one thing."
- "Here's what I can do."
- "Here's what I can't do."
- "I need a moment."

Then choose your move: appreciation, clarity, request, or boundary.

**The "one and done" rule for clarity**

If your trigger is correcting people, you may keep clarifying until you feel understood. That often becomes a debate.

Try this for a week:

Clarify once. Then stop.

Examples: *"To clarify, it's at 6."*

Pause.

If they keep pushing: *"I've clarified my side."*

You're allowed to stop explaining.

**A small checklist for requests**

Before you send a request, check:

- Did I ask in one sentence?
- Did I remove apology padding?
- Did I include a clear timeline if needed?
- Did I keep warmth as a second sentence only?

Then send it.

**If you want to go a bit further: The 5 replacements, written once**

Write these five sentences and keep them where you can see them. They are your defaults.

- *"Quick question."*
- *"Thanks for your patience."*
- *"To clarify, ____."*
- *"Can you ____?"*
- *"That won't work for me."*

Using defaults is not lazy. It's how habits change.

**Final note**

Clarity first. Warmth second. Then stop.

**Take this with you**

- The Replacement Ladder gives you five moves for moments when you're not at fault.
- Remove filler changes your baseline quickly.
- Appreciation works for timing and waiting without self-blame.
- Clarity, requests, and boundaries keep your message accurate and easier to respond to.
- Practice one move at a time and let your message stand.

**Coming up**

Next, you'll learn how to apologize when you truly are wrong, using a simple repair structure that is clear, accountable, and free of self-punishment.

# Chapter 5
# Real Apologies When You're Actually Wrong

If you've apologized for everything, it can feel strange to imagine apologizing less.

A common fear is that reducing reflex apologies will make you less accountable. But accuracy usually does the opposite. When you stop apologizing out of habit, your real apologies become clearer and more meaningful.

This chapter keeps the part of "sorry" that matters. A real apology repairs trust. It acknowledges impact. It shows responsibility without turning into self-punishment.

The goal is not to apologize less at all costs. The goal is to apologize well when it actually fits, and to stop using apology as a way to manage discomfort.

**Start here**

- A real apology is for real wrongdoing or real impact, not for existing.
- The best apologies are specific, calm, and paired with repair.
- Over-explaining and self-attack often derail repair.
- You can acknowledge impact without begging for forgiveness.
- Today you'll learn a simple four-part repair structure and practice it.

**What's really going on**

Chapters 1 to 4 helped you reduce unnecessary apologies and replace them with clearer tools. That works when you are not at fault.

But sometimes you are at fault.

You forgot something. You spoke sharply. You broke an agreement. You made a mistake that affected someone else. You misread the situation and caused harm.

When that happens, a real apology is not weakness. It's responsibility.

The problem is that many over-apologizers apologize in a way that tries to manage the other person's reaction and manage their own anxiety at the same time.

That usually sounds like:

- multiple apologies in a row
- long explanations that sound like defense
- self-attack that shifts the emotional labor to the other person
- a desperate need for reassurance

Those habits don't repair. They often add pressure to the other person.

A clean apology has a job:

- name what happened
- name impact
- offer repair
- show change

That's what you will learn here.

**Easy mistakes to watch for**

- Apologizing for someone's feelings instead of your behavior.
- Saying "sorry" repeatedly without making anything right.
- Explaining first, repairing later.
- Using self-attack as proof you care.
- Trying to force forgiveness.

You can be accountable without collapsing.

### How to do this

Use this four-part structure when you are actually wrong.

### Step 1: Name what you did

Be specific. Avoid vague apologies that make the person guess.

Instead of: *"Sorry about earlier."*
Try: *"I interrupted you when you were speaking."*

### Step 2: Name the impact

Show that you understand how it landed. Keep it calm.

Examples:
- *"That put you on the spot."*
- *"That probably felt dismissive."*
- *"That caused extra stress."*
- *"That undermined trust."*

If you're unsure: *"I can see how that could have felt frustrating."*

### Step 3: Offer repair

Repair answers: what will you do now?

Repair can be practical:

- fix the mistake
- replace something
- follow up with a concrete action
- make a plan for the next step

**Step 4: State the change**

Change is what makes an apology more than a moment.

Examples:

- *"Next time I'll check before I speak."*
- *"I'll set a reminder so I don't forget."*
- *"If I feel irritated, I'll pause before replying."*

You don't need a dramatic promise. You need a realistic change.

**What this looks like in real life**

**Scenario 1: You forgot something important**

You said you'd call someone back. You didn't. They message: *"Did you forget?"*

Your reflex might be: *"I'm so sorry, I feel terrible, I've been so busy, I'm the worst."*

That response apologizes, but it doesn't repair. It also pressures the other person to comfort you. Use the four-part structure.

1) **Name what you did:** *"I didn't call you back yesterday."*
2) **Name impact:** *"I know that likely felt dismissive and frustrating."*
3) **Offer repair:** *"I can call you at 7 tonight or tomorrow morning."*
4) **State change:** *"I'm going to set a reminder as soon as we choose a time."*

Put together:

*"I didn't call you back yesterday. I know that likely felt dismissive and frustrating. I can call you at 7 tonight or tomorrow morning. I'm going to set a reminder as soon as we choose a time."*

That is calm. That is specific. That is repair.

**Scenario 2: You spoke sharply**

Sometimes you don't "mess up a task." You mess up your tone. If you spoke sharply, you can still apologize cleanly.

*"I spoke sharply earlier. That wasn't fair to you. I'm sorry. I'm going to pause next time I feel irritated."*

Notice what you didn't do:

- you didn't defend the tone with a long story
- you didn't attack yourself
- you didn't demand reassurance

You owned it and you changed the pattern.

**Scripts you can use**

These script sets are unique to Chapter 5 and focus on repair language.

**Micro script set 1: Four-part apology starters**

1) *"I need to own something."*
2) *"I got that wrong."*
3) *"I'm sorry for ____."*
4) *"I can see how that affected you."*
5) *"Here's what I'm doing to fix it."*
6) *"Here's what I'll do differently next time."*
7) *"I understand if you're still upset."*
8) *"You don't have to reassure me."*

**Micro script set 2: Repair actions you can offer**

1) *"I can fix this today by ____."*
2) *"I'll replace ____."*
3) *"I'll follow up by ____."*
4) *"I'll take responsibility for ____."*
5) *"I'll confirm the details in writing."*
6) *"I'll set a reminder so it doesn't repeat."*
7) *"I'll make it right by ____."*
8) *"I'll check in after ____ to make sure it's resolved."*

**A quick practice**
**Practice: Two-sentence repair**

Write a two-sentence apology using this structure:

- Sentence 1: what you did and impact
- Sentence 2: repair and change

Example:

*"I canceled last minute and I know that was frustrating. I can reschedule for Friday, and next time I'll confirm earlier."*

Do it once for a real situation or a small past one.

**Try this**
**The Four-Part Repair Script**

**Step 1: Choose one real situation to repair**
Pick something small to medium, where repair is possible.

**Step 2: Write Step 1 in plain language**
"I did X."

**Step 3: Write Step 2 without dramatizing**
"That likely affected you by Y."

**Step 4: Write Step 3 as a concrete action**
"Here's what I'll do to repair it: Z."

**Step 5: Write Step 4 as prevention**
"Here's what I'll do differently next time: A."

**Step 6: Remove self-attack and defense**
Delete "I'm the worst," "I had so much going on," and other lines that shift focus away from repair.

**Step 7: Deliver it once**
Say it or send it. Then stop. Let the other person respond.

**If this feels hard**
**"I want them to know I didn't mean it."**

Intent can matter, but impact still matters. If you want to mention intent, do it after repair, not before.

**"I feel like I need to apologize repeatedly."**

One clean apology with repair usually lands better than many apologies. Repetition can start sounding like panic.

**"What if they don't accept it."**

You can't control acceptance. You can control your ownership and your repair.

**"What if I'm only partly wrong."**

Apologize for your part without taking all the blame: *"I'm sorry I snapped. I should've handled that better. I also want to talk about what led up to it, but I'm owning my part first."*

**The difference between remorse and self-punishment**

A big reason over-apologizers struggle with repair is that they confuse remorse with self-punishment.

Remorse is:

- recognizing impact
- taking responsibility
- fixing what you can
- changing the pattern

Self-punishment is:

- attacking yourself
- begging for reassurance
- making the other person manage your feelings
- repeating "sorry" until you feel relief

Self-punishment can look like caring, but it often makes repair harder. The other person may feel pressured to say "It's okay" even if it isn't.

A clean apology allows space for the other person's feelings without demanding comfort.

If you want a simple line that removes pressure, try: *"You don't have to reassure me. I'm owning it."*

**The one sentence you should avoid**

If you are actually wrong, avoid "I'm sorry you feel that way." It sounds like you're apologizing for their emotions while refusing responsibility.

Instead, name your behavior:

- *"I'm sorry I said that."*
- *"I'm sorry I didn't follow through."*

Then move to repair.

**Scenario 3: You broke a small agreement**

You agreed to do something and you didn't do it. Not a life-ending mistake, but enough to matter.

Old pattern: *"I'm so sorry, I'm terrible, I had so much going on."*

Clean repair: *"I didn't do what I said I'd do. I can see that made things harder for you. I'm doing it now, and next time I'll set a reminder as soon as we agree."*

If you need to offer a choice: *"I can do it tonight or tomorrow morning. Which works for you?"*

This keeps the apology practical and focused on repair.

**Scenario 4: You gave incorrect information**

Sometimes the repair is not emotional. It's factual.

*"I gave you the wrong information. I'm sorry. Here's the correct detail: ____. I'll double-check next time before I share it."*

Short, specific, fixed.

**What to do when the other person wants to keep talking about it**

Some people accept an apology quickly. Others need to talk. If the person wants to talk, your job is to listen without turning the conversation into self-defense.

A simple structure helps:

1) **Acknowledge**: *"I hear you."*
2) **Own**: *"You're right. That wasn't okay."*
3) **Repair**: *"Here's what I'm doing now."*
4) **Change**: *"Here's what will be different."*

Then stop and listen again.

If you notice yourself explaining to reduce your discomfort, return to ownership: *"You're right. I'm owning it."*

**Quick check before you apologize**

Before you apologize, ask:

- Did I cause harm or break an agreement?
- Can I name what I did in one sentence?
- Can I offer one concrete repair?
- Can I state one realistic change?

If yes, you have a clean apology.

**When you're tempted to explain first**

Many over-apologizers start with a long explanation because they fear being judged. The explanation is an attempt to control how you are seen.

The problem is that explanations can sound like excuses when they come before ownership.

A cleaner order is:

1) Own the behavior.
2) Name impact.
3) Offer repair.
4) Add one context sentence only if it helps.
5) State change.

Context belongs after repair, not before.
Here's a quick example.

Not clean: *"I'm sorry I forgot. I've been overwhelmed and I had so many things going on and I didn't sleep well and I wasn't thinking."*

Clean: *"I forgot. I know that affected you. I'm taking care of it now and I'm setting a reminder so it doesn't happen again. I've been overloading my schedule and I'm fixing that."*

The difference is that the person hears ownership first, not a defense.

**The apology types that don't repair**

Some apologies sound polite but don't actually do the job. If you use these, people may feel like nothing was really owned.

**1) The vague apology**

*"Sorry about that."*
This forces the other person to guess what you're apologizing for.
Fix: Name the behavior in one sentence.

**2) The conditional apology**

*"Sorry if I upset you."*
This implies the harm might not be real.
Fix: *"I'm sorry I said that."*

**3) The emotion-only apology**

*"I'm sorry you're upset."*
This centers their feelings and dodges your behavior.
Fix: *"I'm sorry I did ____."*

**4) The apology that demands reassurance**

*"I'm the worst. Please don't be mad."*
This shifts the labor to the other person.
Fix: *"You don't have to reassure me. I'm owning it."*

**5) The apology that repeats without change**

If you keep apologizing for the same behavior but don't change anything, trust drops. Repair needs a change plan, even a small one.

**The two-sentence repair you can use in most situations**

If you want a simple version of the four-part structure, use this:

- Sentence 1: Behavior plus impact.
- Sentence 2: Repair plus change.

Examples:

- *"I canceled last minute and I know that was frustrating. I can reschedule for Friday and I'll confirm earlier next time."*
- *"I spoke sharply and that wasn't fair. I'm sorry. I'm going to pause before responding next time."*
- *"I forgot and I can see that affected you. I'm handling it now and I'll set a reminder so it doesn't repeat."*

This keeps you accountable without turning the apology into a speech.

**What this looks like in real life**

Here are two common repair moments that aren't about tasks, but about tone, misunderstanding, and shutdown.

**Scenario 5: Partly wrong, partly misunderstood**

Sometimes you did something wrong, but there's also a misunderstanding. The mistake is trying to solve both at once.

A clean approach is to own your part first, then address the misunderstanding later.

Example: *"I'm sorry I snapped. That wasn't okay. I'm going to slow down next time I feel irritated. After that, I'd like to clarify what I meant, because I think we misunderstood each other."*

This keeps repair clean and prevents your clarification from sounding like a defense.

**Scenario 6: When the other person doesn't want to talk**

Sometimes you apologize and the person says, "Whatever," or "Fine," and goes quiet.

Your reflex may be to chase them with more apologies to get closure.

Instead, keep it simple:

*"I understand. I'm here when you're ready to talk. I'm still owning what I did."*

Then stop.

Your apology is not a transaction. You can offer repair without forcing a response.

**Scripts you can use add-on: Clean lines for tough moments**

Use these when your anxiety wants to take over.

1) *"You don't have to reassure me. I'm owning it."*
2) *"I'm not making excuses. I'm taking responsibility."*
3) *"I understand if you're still upset."*
4) *"Here's what I'm doing to fix it."*
5) *"I can see the impact clearly now."*
6) *"I'm listening. Go ahead."*
7) *"I'm going to do better by changing ____."*
8) *"I'm going to give you space, and I'll follow through."*

**Repair is a plan, not a performance**

If you grew up thinking apologies were about saying the right emotional words, you might feel pressure to sound intensely remorseful. But most people don't need drama. They need reliability.

A repair plan answers three practical questions:

- What is happening now?
- What will you do next?
- What will be different?

When your apology includes those three things, you reduce uncertainty, which is often what hurts most.

**What makes an apology believable**

Believability usually comes from specifics, not intensity.

*Specifics include:*
- naming the behavior clearly
- naming the impact in normal language
- offering a concrete repair
- stating a realistic change
- following through

*Intensity includes:*
- repeating "sorry" many times
- self-attack
- begging for reassurance
- dramatic statements like "I'll never forgive myself"

Intensity can feel sincere, but it often creates pressure. Specifics create trust.

**When you should apologize even if you didn't mean it**

Intent matters, but it's not the same as impact. You can cause harm without meaning to. A clean apology is still appropriate when:

- your tone was sharp
- your words landed as dismissive
- you broke an agreement, even accidentally
- your action caused stress or inconvenience that you could reasonably have prevented

You do not need to apologize for being human. You do need to apologize for harm you caused, even unintentionally.

If you want a simple line that holds both truths: *"I didn't mean to hurt you, and I can see that I did. I'm sorry."*

Then move to repair and change.

**Scenario 5: You forgot, and the person is still angry**

They say: *"This is the third time."*

Your reflex may be to explain why it happened. But the person already knows you have reasons. They want reliability.

Clean response: *"You're right. I didn't follow through, and I can see why you're angry. I'm fixing it today. I'm also changing my system so it doesn't repeat, starting with a reminder and a smaller commitment."*

This includes ownership, impact, repair, and change. It also shows you heard the pattern.

**Scenario 6: You said something hurtful in a joking tone**

You might want to defend with: *"I was joking."*

A cleaner approach: *"I said that as a joke, and it landed as hurtful. I'm sorry. I won't make jokes like that about you again."*

If you want to repair: *"Is there anything you need from me right now?"*

Keep the question simple. Then listen.

**The listening part of repair**

Some apologies fail because the apologizer talks the whole time. If the person wants to tell you how it felt, your job is not to correct their feelings. Your job is to listen.

Try this three-line response:

- *"I hear you."*
- *"You're right. That wasn't okay."*
- *"Thank you for telling me."*

Then stop. Let them speak.

If you're tempted to explain, return to ownership: *"I'm owning it."*

**If you want to go a bit further: Build your personal repair script**

If you want to become consistent, write one repair script you can adapt to most situations. Keep it in your notes.

Template:

*"I did ____. I can see that affected you by ____. Here's what I'm doing to repair it: ____. Here's what I'll do differently next time: ____."*

Then shorten it into two sentences:

*"I did ____, and I can see the impact. I'm repairing it by ____ and I'll change ____ so it doesn't repeat."*

This keeps your apology from turning into a ramble when you're nervous.

**Quick check before you hit send**

Before you send an apology, check:

- Did I name what I did?
- Did I name impact without dramatizing?
- Did I offer a concrete repair?
- Did I state one realistic change?
- Did I avoid self-attack and reassurance-seeking?

If yes, send it once and stop.

**Closing reminder**

A clean apology does not erase the moment. It starts repair. The follow-through is what finishes it.

**If you want to go a bit further: Repair when the other person is also wrong**

Sometimes both people contributed to a situation. The mistake is using that fact to dodge your part.

A clean approach:

1) Own your part first.
2) Repair your part.
3) Then address the other part later, when the moment is calmer.

Example: *"I'm sorry I snapped. That wasn't okay. I'm going to slow down next time. I also want to talk about how we were speaking to each other, but I'm owning my part first."*

This keeps your apology credible and prevents it from turning into a debate.

### A short menu for common repairs

Use one of these when you need a quick repair action.

- **Missed message**: *"I missed this. I'm responding now and I'll set a reminder next time."*
- **Late arrival**: *"I'm late and I know that affected you. I'm here now and I'll plan more buffer next time."*
- **Broken plan**: *"I didn't follow through. I'm fixing it by ____ and I'll change ____ so it doesn't repeat."*
- **Hurtful comment**: *"I said ____. That was hurtful. I'm sorry and I won't repeat it."*
- **Overstep**: *"I crossed a line. I'm sorry. I'll check with you before I do that again."*

### Final scenario: When you need to apologize to yourself

If you're used to self-attack, you might keep punishing yourself after you apologize to someone else. That doesn't improve repair. It just drains you.

Try a cleaner internal line, one that keeps accountability without turning it into self-attack.

Use one of these:

- *"I owned it. I repaired what I could. I'm done punishing myself."*
- *"I can learn from this without attacking myself."*
- *"I made a mistake. I'm fixing it. I'm moving on."*
- *"I don't need to feel worse to be better."*

If you want a simple two-step reset, do this in under a minute:

- Name the lesson in one sentence: *"Next time, I will ____."*
- Name the follow-through in one sentence: *"Today, I will ____."*

Example:
Next time, I will pause before I reply.
Today, I will send the follow-up message and set a reminder.

That's self-respect plus repair. No extra punishment required.

**Take this with you**

- Real apologies are for real wrongdoing or impact, not for discomfort.
- A clean apology names behavior and impact, then offers repair and change.
- Over-explaining and self-attack often derail repair.
- You can be accountable without begging for reassurance.
- Practice two-sentence repair to build the habit.

**Coming up**

Next, you'll learn how to set boundaries without apology padding, so you can say no and ask for what you need without turning it into guilt or negotiation.

# CHAPTER 6
# BOUNDARIES WITHOUT SORRY

If you've relied on apology to keep things smooth, boundaries can feel like a threat.

Not because boundaries are aggressive, but because they remove your usual safety tools. You can't cushion a limit with five apologies and still call it a limit. You can't say no while begging the other person not to be disappointed.

So many people do one of two things:

- avoid boundaries until resentment builds
- set a boundary, then backtrack with explanations until the boundary disappears

This chapter is about a third option: calm boundaries that are clear, kind, and free of apology padding.

**Start here**

- A boundary is information, not a debate.
- Apology padding turns boundaries into negotiations.
- The clearest boundaries are short, steady, and repeated calmly.
- Warmth can stay without self-blame.
- Today you'll build a neutral boundary script and practice it.

**What's really going on**

By now you can see the difference between unnecessary apology and real repair. You can map triggers, use one sentence first, and choose ladder moves instead of reflex sorry. You can also apologize well when you are actually wrong.

Now we apply those skills to one of the biggest "sorry traps" of all: boundaries.

A boundary is a clear statement of:

- what you will do
- what you will not do
- what you are available for
- what you are not available for
- what behavior you will accept
- what behavior you will not accept

Boundaries are not punishments. They are not threats. They are not moral lectures. They are practical limits that protect your time, energy, and self-respect.

### Why over-apologizers struggle with boundaries

Over-apologizers often learned that being liked requires being easy. If that was rewarded, apology became a way to keep your limits invisible.

So, when you try to set a boundary, your system may interpret it as risk:

- they will be mad
- they will think I'm selfish
- they will pull away
- I will look rude
- I will have to defend myself

That fear is the trigger.

The reflex is to apologize and explain.

But here's the problem:

An apology inside a boundary often turns the boundary into a request for approval.

If you say: *"Sorry, I can't"*

and then add a long story, many people hear: "If you push, I might change."

The goal of this chapter is to help your boundary sound settled while still sounding human.

**The Calm Boundary Formula**

Boundary statement + optional warmth + optional next step.

That's it.

Examples:

- *"I can't do tonight. Thanks for understanding."*

- *"That won't work for me. I can do Thursday instead."*

- *"I'm not comfortable with that. Please don't ask again."*

The boundary comes first. Warmth is optional. A next step is optional.

**Easy mistakes to watch for**

- Over-explaining your boundary so it sounds negotiable.
- Adding apology padding that signals guilt.
- Offering alternatives you don't actually want.
- Backtracking when the other person reacts.
- Turning a boundary into a debate about fairness.

If you want one simple rule:

If you say no, do not keep talking to make it feel better.

**How to do this**

**Step 1: Choose the boundary type**

Most boundaries fall into one of these categories:

- Time boundary: how much time you can give
- Availability boundary: when you are accessible
- Request boundary: what you can and cannot do for others
- Conversation boundary: what you will discuss and what you won't
- Behavior boundary: how you expect to be treated

Choose the type first. It helps you pick the right words.

**Step 2: Write the boundary statement in one sentence**

Common boundary starters:

- *"I can't ____."*
- *"I'm not available ____."*
- *"That won't work for me."*
- *"I'm not comfortable with ____."*
- *"Please don't ____."*

Keep it short. Short is not rude. Short is clear.

**Step 3: Add optional warmth without guilt**

Warmth lines that keep your boundary intact:

- *"Thanks for understanding."*
- *"I appreciate you asking."*
- *"I know that's disappointing."*
- *"I hope it goes well."*

Avoid warmth that turns into self-blame:

- *"I feel terrible."*
- *"I'm the worst."*
- *"I'm so sorry I'm like this."*

**Step 4: Add a next step only if it's real**

Alternatives are optional. Use them only if you actually want them.

Good alternatives are specific:

- *"I can do Thursday instead."*
- *"I can help for 20 minutes tomorrow."*
- *"I can talk at 7, not now."*

Avoid vague alternatives that reopen negotiation:

- *"Maybe later"* if you don't mean it
- *"We'll see"* if you know it won't happen

**Step 5: Stop and let the boundary stand**

This is the hard part. Over-apologizers want to keep talking to manage the other person's reaction.

A boundary gets stronger when you stop.

If you need to hold it, you repeat the same sentence.

**What this looks like in real life**

**Scenario 1: Declining a request without a story**

Someone asks: *"Can you help me this weekend?"*

You feel guilty. You don't want to be difficult. Your reflex wants to apologize and explain why you can't.

Old pattern:
*"I'm so sorry. I feel terrible. I've just been exhausted and I have so much going on."*

Clean boundary using the formula:
*"I can't help this weekend. Thanks for understanding."*

If you want to offer a real alternative:
*"I can't help this weekend. I can check in next week."*

If they push:
*"I hear you. I still can't help this weekend."*

Notice how the message stays stable.
The boundary stays calm.

**Scenario 2: A conversation boundary**

Sometimes you need a boundary around a topic or a tone.

If someone keeps pushing a topic you don't want to discuss, your reflex may be to apologize for having that limit.

Clean boundary:
*"I'm not discussing that."*

Optional warmth:
*"I know it matters to you. I'm still not discussing it."*

If it stays tense:
*"I'm going to pause this conversation. We can talk later."*

A conversation boundary protects your energy and prevents spirals.

**Scripts you can use**

These script sets are unique to Chapter 6 and focus on neutral boundary language.

**Micro script set 1: Neutral no lines**

1) *"That won't work for me."*
2) *"I can't do that."*
3) *"I'm not available."*
4) *"I'm going to pass."*
5) *"I'm not comfortable with that."*
6) *"Please don't do that."*
7) *"I'm not discussing this."*
8) *"I'm going to pause this conversation."*

**Micro script set 2: Warm boundaries with one-line kindness**

1) *"Thanks for understanding."*
2) *"I appreciate you asking."*
3) *"I hope it goes well."*
4) *"I know that's disappointing."*
5) *"I can see why you'd ask."*
6) *"I care about this."*
7) *"I want to keep this respectful."*
8) *"I'm saying this to protect our relationship."*

**A quick practice**
**Practice: One low-stakes boundary today**

Choose a small boundary that won't create major fallout. Use a one-sentence boundary statement, then stop.

Examples:

- *"I can't talk right now."*
- *"I'm not available tonight."*
- *"That won't work for me."*

If you want warmth, add one line, then stop.

Afterward, write one receipt:
*"I set a boundary without apologizing."*

**Try this**

**Build Your Neutral No**

**Step 1: Pick one boundary you avoid**
Be specific. Example: *"I'm not available for last-minute plans."*

**Step 2: Choose your neutral no sentence**
Pick one: *"That won't work for me," "I can't do that," "I'm not available," "I'm going to pass."*

**Step 3: Add one warmth line**
Choose one: *"Thanks for understanding," "I appreciate you asking," "I hope it goes well."*

**Step 4: Choose one repeat line for pushback**
Examples:

- *"My answer is still no."*
- *"That still doesn't work for me."*
- *"I'm not changing my mind."*

**Step 5: Choose one exit line**
Examples:

- *"I'm going to pause this."*
- *"I'm not discussing this further."*

**Step 6: Practice out loud**
Say the boundary sentence three times. Say the repeat line twice. Say the exit line once.

**Step 7: Choose one small practice moment this week**
Use a smaller version of your boundary in a low-stakes moment.

**If this feels hard**

**"Boundaries make me feel selfish."**

A boundary is how you manage your life. You can be kind and still have limits.

If you want a reminder:
Saying no prevents resentment.

**"They keep asking why."**

You don't owe a courtroom-level explanation.

Try: *"I'm not available."*

If they push: *"I'm not discussing it."*

**"I keep offering alternatives I don't want."**

That is discomfort talking. Only offer alternatives you truly want.

**"I set the boundary and now I feel guilty."**

Guilt isn't always a sign you did something wrong. Sometimes it's a sign you did something new.

Ask: *"Was I clear and respectful?"*

If yes, let it stand.

**The difference between a boundary and a preference**

Some people avoid boundaries because they think boundaries must be dramatic. They don't. But it helps to know what you're saying.

A preference is flexible: *"I'd rather do Thursday."*

A boundary is settled: *"I can't do Thursday."*

If you treat boundaries like preferences, you'll feel pulled into negotiation. If you treat preferences like boundaries, you might sound rigid.

A quick check:

- If you can flex, it's a preference.
- If you can't flex without resentment, it's a boundary.

**Scenario 3: Time boundary without apology**

Someone wants to talk right now and you don't have capacity.

Old pattern: *"Sorry, I can't talk right now, I feel bad."*

Clean boundary: *"I can't talk right now. I can talk at 7."*

Optional warmth: *"Thanks for understanding."*

You gave a clear no and a clear next step.

**How to hold a boundary when you feel pressured**

Pressure often shows up as repetition. The person asks again, or they challenge your reason, or they use guilt.

Your goal is not to convince them. Your goal is to hold the boundary.

Use this three-step pattern:

1) reflect briefly: *"I hear you."*
2) repeat the boundary: *"I still can't do that."*
3) stop talking

If it keeps going, use an exit line:
*"I'm going to pause this conversation."*

Short repetition is often kinder than a long debate.

**If you want to go a bit further: The two sentence boundary rule**

If you tend to over-explain, try this for one week.

Sentence 1: the boundary.
Sentence 2: warmth or next step.

Examples:
- *"I can't do tonight. I hope it goes well."*
- *"That won't work for me. Thanks for understanding."*
- *"I'm not discussing that. We can talk about something else."*

Then stop. If you need to repeat, repeat sentence 1 only.

**Quick check before you answer**

Before you respond to a request, ask:

- Do I actually want to do this?
- Will I resent it if I say yes?
- What is the cleanest no I can say?

Then use the boundary sentence and stop.

**Why boundaries trigger guilt in the first place**

Guilt is one of the main reasons people keep apologizing inside boundaries.

It helps to separate three kinds of guilt.

**1) True guilt**

True guilt is a signal you violated your own values. You harmed someone, broke an agreement, or acted unfairly. True guilt is useful because it guides repair.

**2) Role guilt**

Role guilt happens when you step out of a role you've played for a long time. If you've been the easy one, the helper, the fixer, the person who never says no, then saying no can feel wrong even when it's reasonable.

Role guilt is not proof you did something bad. It's proof you changed the pattern.

### 3) Discomfort guilt

Discomfort guilt is the feeling that shows up when someone else is disappointed, annoyed, or unhappy and you don't rush to fix it.

If you've used apology to smooth emotions, then not smoothing can feel unsafe. Again, that isn't proof you did something wrong. It's your nervous system learning a new skill.

A helpful internal line is: "Guilt is not always a moral signal. Sometimes it's a habit signal."

### The boundary doesn't need permission

Many over-apologizers treat boundaries like requests. They present the boundary, then wait for approval.

A boundary isn't: *"Is it okay if I don't?"*
A boundary is: *"I can't."*

Approval is nice. It's not required.

You can still be respectful. You can still show care. But you're not required to ask permission to have limits.

### Scenario 4: Behavior boundary without escalation

Someone makes a comment that feels disrespectful.

You feel the urge to apologize for reacting, or to laugh it off so the moment passes.

Clean boundary: *"Please don't speak to me like that."*

Optional warmth: *"I'm happy to keep talking, just not in that tone."*

If they respond with *"I was joking,"* you don't need to argue: *"I hear you. I still need you not to speak to me that way."*

Behavior boundaries are where apology padding causes the most damage, because it teaches people your dignity is negotiable.

**Scenario 5: The boundary you set and then undo**

This is a common pattern.

You say: *"I can't do Saturday."*

Then you feel guilty, and you send: *"Sorry, I feel terrible, I just have so much going on, maybe I can try to make it work."*

What happened is that the boundary triggered discomfort guilt. The follow-up apology is an attempt to get relief.

Try a different response plan:

- set the boundary
- pause ten minutes
- if you still want to add something, add only a real alternative, not guilt

Example: *"I can't do Saturday. I can do Tuesday instead."*

No self-blame. No performance. Just information.

**Scripts you can use add-on: Repeat lines for boundaries**

Use these when someone pushes.

1) *"That still doesn't work for me."*
2) *"My answer is still no."*
3) *"I hear you. I still can't."*
4) *"I understand. I'm not changing my mind."*
5) *"I can't do that, and I'm not debating it."*
6) *"I've answered, and my answer is the same."*
7) *"I'm going to pause this conversation now."*
8) *"We can talk later when it's calmer."*

These lines protect you from being pulled into explanations.

**When people use guilt tactics**

Not everyone pushes boundaries in the same way. Some people are direct. Others use guilt, sarcasm, or withdrawal.

Here are common guilt tactics and clean responses.

**Tactic: *"After all I've done for you"***

Clean response: *"I hear you. I still can't do that."*

If you want to add one line: *"I'm not trading favors. I'm not available."*

**Tactic: *"If you cared, you would"***

Clean response: *"I do care. My answer is still no."*

**Tactic: *"You've changed"***

Clean response: *"Yes, I'm being clearer."*

**Tactic: *"You're selfish"***

Clean response: *"I'm okay with you seeing it that way. I'm still not doing it."*

You're not agreeing with the label. You're refusing to debate your boundary.

**Tactic: Silent treatment**

The urge is to chase with apologies to restore connection.

A cleaner move: *"I'm here when you're ready to talk calmly."*

Then stop.

You do not need to earn connection by abandoning your limits.

**The boundary ladder inside the boundary ladder**

Sometimes you don't know if a moment requires a preference, a request, or a boundary.

Use this quick internal ladder:

1) Preference: *"I'd rather ____."*
2) Request: *"Can we ____."*
3) Boundary: *"I can't ____."*

Start with the least intense option that is still honest.

If you truly can't, go straight to boundary. If you can flex, try preference or request.

This keeps your communication proportional.

**A practical method: The boundary statement stack**

When you're new to boundaries, it helps to stack your boundary in a predictable order.

1) boundary: *"I can't do that."*
2) optional warmth: *"Thanks for understanding."*
3) optional alternative: *"I can do ____ instead."*
4) repeat line if pushed: *"That still doesn't work for me."*
5) exit if needed: *"I'm going to pause this conversation."*

You don't have to use every line. You just need to know the order.

**A quick practice add-on**

If you're worried about being too abrupt, practice boundaries in places where the relationship is low stakes.

Examples:

- decline an upsell politely
- say no to a minor request
- set a time limit on a call

Every low-stakes rep builds your ability to hold boundaries in higher-stakes relationships.

### Exercise add-on: Boundary scripts for your top 3 situations

If you want your boundaries to work under pressure, pre-write them for the exact situations you face most. This keeps you from improvising while anxious.

**Step 1: Write your three situations**
Examples:

- last-minute plan requests
- being asked for favors you don't want to do
- someone pushing a topic you won't discuss

**Step 2: Write a boundary sentence for each**
Examples:

- *"I'm not available for last-minute plans."*
- *"I can't help with that."*
- *"I'm not discussing that."*

**Step 3: Add one warmth line for each** (Choose one)

- *"Thanks for understanding."*
- *"I appreciate you asking."*
- *"I hope it goes well."*

**Step 4: Add one repeat line**
*"My answer is still no."*

**Step 5: Add one exit line**
*"I'm going to pause this conversation."*

**Step 6: Practice out loud**
Say each boundary once, slowly. Then stop.

This practice matters because boundaries fail most often at the first pushback. Pre-written repeat lines protect you.

**A final mindset shift**

Boundaries are not something you do to other people. They are something you do for yourself.

They are a way of saying:

- This is what I can do.
- This is what I can't do.
- This is what I will accept.
- This is what I won't accept.
- That's not rude. It's honest.

**The "second no" is the real boundary**

Most people can say no once. The hard part is holding no when the other person reacts.

That's why the second no matters more than the first.

Here's what the second no looks like.

First no: *"I can't do Saturday."*

Pushback: *"Come on, it's only two hours."*

Second no: *"I hear you. I still can't do Saturday."*

That's not cold. It's stable.

If you add new reasons every time you repeat, you create new debate points. If you repeat the same sentence, the conversation either ends or becomes clearly about the other person's inability to accept your limit.

**Scenario 6: Setting a time limit instead of a full no**

Some boundaries don't need to be a full refusal. They need a limit.

Example: *"I can talk for 15 minutes, then I have to go."*

If the person ignores the limit, use the second no: *"I have to go now."*

Then go.

Time boundaries are where many people apologize themselves into staying longer than they want. A clean limit protects you without drama.

**Scenario 7: When you want to help but not rescue**

Sometimes you do want to support someone. You just don't want to become responsible for everything.

Try this format: *"I can help with ____ for ____ minutes. I can't do the whole thing."*

This is a boundary that keeps your care intact.

Example: *"I can help you brainstorm for 20 minutes. I can't take over the project."*

This is honest, kind, and protective.

### Quick check before you say yes

If you're deciding whether to say yes, ask:

- Do I have the capacity?
- Will I resent this later?
- Am I saying yes to avoid tension?
- If I said no, what am I afraid would happen?

If the fear is the main reason, you probably need a boundary.

### Take this with you

- Boundaries are information, not debates.
- Apology padding often turns no into negotiation.
- Use the Calm Boundary Formula: boundary, optional warmth, optional next step.
- Repeat calmly instead of defending your boundary.
- Practice low-stakes boundaries to build confidence.

### Coming up

Next, you'll learn how to handle pushback and guilt tactics without backtracking or slipping into over-explaining.

# CHAPTER 7
# HANDLING PUSHBACK AND HIGH-TRIGGER PEOPLE

It's one thing to practice clearer language when everyone is calm. It's another thing to use it when someone is disappointed, critical, impatient, or persistent.

Pushback is where many people slide back into old habits. A boundary becomes a debate. A request becomes an apology. A clean sentence becomes a long explanation.

This chapter is about staying steady when someone pushes.

Not by becoming harsh. Not by winning. By holding your message with calm repetition, simple pauses, and clean exits when needed.

## Start here

- Pushback is common and doesn't automatically mean you did something wrong.
- A pause gives you choice when your reflex wants to apologize or explain.
- Repetition is a skill, not rudeness.
- You don't need agreement for your boundary to be valid.
- Today you'll build a pushback plan: pause, reflect, repeat, exit.

## What's really going on

Chapters 1 through 6 gave you tools to replace reflex apologies, speak cleanly, use the Replacement Ladder, apologize well when needed, and set boundaries without apology padding.

Now you need one more skill: staying steady when someone reacts. Pushback can be obvious:

- *"Come on, just do it."*
- *"Why are you being like this?"*

It can also be subtle:

- *"Wow. Okay."*
- *"I guess I'll just do everything myself."*
- *"You've changed."*

If you've used apology and over-explaining to keep the peace, pushback can feel like an alarm. Your nervous system wants to restore calm fast, and "sorry" is the old tool.

Here's the key truth that helps you stay grounded: *Pushback isn't proof your boundary is wrong. Pushback is often proof your boundary is new.*

Your job isn't to make pushback disappear. Your job is to communicate clearly and stop when the conversation becomes circular or disrespectful.

**Easy mistakes to watch for**

- Over-explaining to earn permission.
- Apologizing to make discomfort stop.
- Matching intensity when someone escalates.
- Trying to get them to accept your boundary.
- Staying in the conversation too long.

You can be calm and still be firm.

**How to do this**

Use this pressure plan > *Pause. Reflect. Repeat. Exit.*

**Step 1: Pause**

The pause interrupts autopilot. It can be one breath or one line.

Pause lines:

- *"Give me a second. I want to answer clearly."*
- *"Let me think for a moment."*
- *"I need a minute."*

The pause is not avoidance. It's a choice.

**Step 2: Reflect**

Reflection acknowledges emotion without surrendering your position.

Reflection lines:

- *"I hear you."*
- *"I get that this is frustrating."*
- *"I can see you were hoping for a different answer."*

Reflection is not agreement. It's acknowledgment.

**Step 3: Repeat**

Repeat is the broken record skill.

You restate your boundary without adding new information.

Repeat lines:

- *"My answer is still no."*
- *"That doesn't work for me."*
- *"I still can't do that."*

Repetition keeps you out of debate.

**Step 4: Exit**

Exit is for when the conversation becomes circular, disrespectful, or draining.

Exit lines:

- *"I'm going to pause this conversation."*
- *"I'm not discussing this further."*
- *"We can talk later when we're calmer."*
- *"I'm going to end this call now."*

Exiting is not rude. It's a boundary.

**What this looks like in real life**

**Scenario 1: Guilt-based pushback**

A friend asks: *"Can you come with me tonight? I don't want to go alone."*

You need rest. You say: *"I can't tonight. I hope it goes well."*

They push: *"Seriously. I always show up for you."*

Use the pressure plan.

Pause: *"Give me a second. I want to answer clearly."*

Reflect: *"I get that you don't want to go alone."*

Repeat: *"I still can't tonight."*

Optional next step, only if real: *"I can check in with you earlier tomorrow."*

If they escalate: *"Wow. I guess I know where I stand."*

Reflect: *"I hear that you're upset."*

Repeat: *"I'm still not going tonight."*

Exit if needed: *"I'm going to pause this conversation. We can talk tomorrow."*

You stayed kind. You stayed clear. You did not negotiate your rest.

**Scenario 2: The high-trigger person**

A high-trigger person is anyone who reliably activates your old pattern. They might be blunt, critical, unpredictable, or prone to guilt tactics.

The goal is not to change them. The goal is to keep your footing.

A useful rule:

If someone consistently pulls you into over-explaining, shorten your responses.

Shorter responses reduce debate points and reduce your own anxiety.

### Scripts you can use

These script sets are unique to Chapter 7 and focus on handling pushback.

### Micro script set 1: Pushback responses

1) *"I hear you. My answer is still no."*
2) *"I get it. That still doesn't work for me."*
3) *"I understand. I'm not changing my mind."*
4) *"I'm not debating this."*
5) *"I've answered. My answer is the same."*
6) *"I'm going to pause this now."*
7) *"We can talk later when it's calmer."*
8) *"I'm going to end the conversation now."*

### Micro script set 2: Calm reflection lines

1) *"I hear you."*
2) *"That makes sense."*
3) *"I get that this is frustrating."*
4) *"I can see why you'd feel that way."*
5) *"I can see you were hoping for a different answer."*
6) *"Thanks for telling me."*
7) *"I'm listening."*
8) *"I want to keep this calm."*

**A quick practice**
**Practice: Build your one-line repeat**

Pick one boundary you're practicing. Write one repeat line that you can say under stress.

Examples:

- *"That doesn't work for me."*
- *"My answer is still no."*
- *"I still can't do that."*

Practice saying it five times slowly.

**Try this**

**The Pushback Plan**

Step 1: Write your boundary sentence.
Step 2: Predict three pushback lines you might hear.
Step 3: Write one reflection line for each pushback line.
Step 4: Write one repeat line you will use every time.
Step 5: Write one exit line.
Step 6: Practice the sequence out loud once.
Step 7: Use it once in a low-stakes moment this week.

**If this feels hard**

**"Repetition feels rude."**

Repetition isn't rudeness. It's clarity. You're not refusing to listen. You're refusing to debate.

**“I start explaining without realizing.”**

Return to the repeat line. The repeat line is your anchor.

**“They escalate and I freeze.”**

If you freeze, use the exit line. You don’t have to keep talking when you’re overwhelmed.

**The Pressure Plan in detail**

Pause. Reflect. Repeat. Exit is the core. Here is how to use it in real time.

**Pause**

Pause is how you prevent your reflex from driving your mouth. You can pause with breath, silence, or a line.

If you freeze, use a restart line:

*“Give me a second.”*
*“I want to answer clearly.”*

**Reflect**

Reflection is a short acknowledgement of their experience.

Use reflection for two reasons:

- it lowers intensity
- it prevents you from sounding cold

Reflection isn't:
*"I'm sorry you feel that way."*

Reflection is:
*"I hear you."*
*"I get that this is frustrating."*

**Repeat**

Repeat is a restatement without new reasons.

This is important. If you give new reasons every time, you create new debate points.

Bad repeat: *"I can't because I'm tired, and also because I have a lot going on, and also because..."*

Good repeat: *"I still can't."*

**Exit**

Exit is a boundary around the conversation itself.

Exit is appropriate when:

- the conversation is circular
- the tone is disrespectful
- you feel pressured and flooded
- the person won't accept a clear answer

Exit line plus action: *"I'm going to pause this conversation."* Then pause. *"I'm going to end this call."* Then end it.

Exit isn't a threat. It's self-management.

**The five pushback styles**

Pushback has patterns. When you can name the style, you can respond without taking it personally.

**Style 1: The negotiator**

They keep offering alternatives to your no until you say yes.

They may say:
*"Just this once."*
*"It'll only take an hour."*

Your response:
Reflect, then repeat: *"I hear you. I still can't."*

**Style 2: The guilt drop**

They imply you are bad if you hold your boundary.

They may say:
*"After all I've done."*
*"If you cared, you would."*

Your response:
*"I do care. My answer is still no."*

No debate. No defense speech.

**Style 3: The intensity spike**

They raise their voice, get sharp, or escalate quickly.

Your response:
Pause and exit: *"I'm going to pause this. We can talk later."*

**Style 4: The victim script**

They frame your boundary as you harming them.

They may say:
*"I guess I'll do it alone."*

Your response:
Reflect, then repeat: *"I get that you're upset. I still can't."*

**Style 5: The cold withdrawal**

They go silent or sarcastic to punish your boundary.

Your response:
Don't chase with apologies. Offer calm availability: *"I'm here when you want to talk calmly."*

Then stop.

**Scenario 3: A guilt drop from someone close**

They say: *"If you cared, you'd do this for me."*

Old pattern: You apologize and give in, or you over-explain your reasons until you feel exhausted.

Clean plan:

Pause: *"Give me a second."*

Reflect: *"I hear that you're upset."*

Repeat: *"I still can't do it."*

Optional warmth: *"I care about you. I still can't."*

Then stop.

You're allowed to care without surrendering your limit.

**Scenario 4: Pushback after a clean request**

You ask: *"Can you send the form by tonight?"*

They reply: *"Why are you being so demanding?"*

Clean plan:

Reflect: *"I hear you."*

Clarity: *"I'm asking because I need it to finish my part."*

Offer a choice: *"If tonight doesn't work, tell me when you can send it."*

Then stop.

This protects your request without apology padding.

**Scenario 5: Pushback that turns into character attacks**

They say:
*"You're selfish."*
*"You're difficult."*

Your job isn't to defend your identity. Your job is to hold your boundary.

Response: *"I'm not debating labels. My answer is still no."*
If it continues: *"I'm going to pause this conversation."*

This keeps you out of an endless argument about who you are.

**Scripts you can use add-on: Repeat and exit lines**

1) *"That still doesn't work for me."*
2) *"My answer is still no."*
3) *"I hear you. I still can't."*
4) *"I understand. I'm not changing my mind."*
5) *"I'm not debating this."*
6) *"I'm going to pause this now."*
7) *"We can talk later when we're calmer."*
8) *"I'm going to end the conversation."*

**A quick practice add-on: One pause per day**

Once per day, practice pausing instead of smoothing.

- pause one breath
- choose one reflection line
- speak one boundary sentence

Then stop.

This builds tolerance for discomfort, which is the real skill behind holding boundaries.

**Exercise add-on: Your pushback script for one high-trigger person**

Step 1: Choose one person who triggers you.
Step 2: Write your one sentence boundary.
Step 3: Write three pushback lines you expect.
Step 4: Write one reflection line for each.
Step 5: Write one repeat line you will use every time.
Step 6: Write one exit line.
Step 7: Practice once out loud.
Step 8: Use it once in a low-stakes situation.

You're building a plan, not winning an argument.

**The difference between empathy and surrender**

Empathy is acknowledging a feeling. Surrender is abandoning your position to make the feeling go away.

Empathy: *"I get that you're disappointed."*
Surrender: *"Okay fine, I'll do it."*

When you're new to boundaries, your nervous system may treat empathy as unsafe because it fears conflict. But empathy often lowers intensity and makes your repeat line easier to say.

Use this simple structure:

- empathy sentence
- boundary sentence
- stop

Example: *"I get that you're disappointed. I still can't do tonight."*

**When you get pulled into explaining**

Explaining is not always wrong. The problem is when explanation becomes a defense speech.

A clean guideline:

- One sentence of context is enough.
- If you need more, ask what information they actually need.

Example: *"I can't tonight. I've got a full evening."*

If they ask why: *"I'm not getting into details. I'm still not available."*

This protects you from being interrogated into surrender.

**Scenario 6: The pushback loop in text messages**

Text messages can create a pushback loop because you can keep replying.

They ask: *"Can you do it?"*

You say: *"I can't."*

They reply: *"Why not?"*

Old pattern: You write a long paragraph of reasons.

Clean plan: Use a repeat line:
*"That still doesn't work for me."*

If they continue:
*"I'm going to pause this conversation."*

Then stop replying for a while.

Silence is not rudeness. Silence is you refusing to debate.

**A 24-hour rule for high-trigger conversations**

If a conversation repeatedly escalates, give yourself a rule: I will not resolve this in one sitting.

You can say:
*"I'm not going to solve this right now. I'll talk tomorrow."*

This protects you from panic-compromising your boundaries just to end the tension.

**Quick check before you respond to pushback**

Before you respond, ask:

- Am I trying to prevent anger or rejection?
- Will this response add new debate points?
- Can I repeat my one sentence instead?

Most of the time, the best response is the repeat line you already chose.

**If you want to go a bit further: The three-line response**

When you feel flooded, limit yourself to three lines.

1) Reflect: *"I hear you."*
2) Repeat: *"That doesn't work for me."*
3) Exit: *"I'm going to pause this now."*

Three lines is enough to hold your boundary and protect your nervous system.

**What to do after the conversation**

Over-apologizers often replay pushback for hours. A short debrief helps you learn without spiraling.

1) What pushback style showed up?
2) What trigger did it hit in me?
3) Did I pause, reflect, repeat, or exit?
4) What line worked best?
5) What will I say next time?

Write two sentences, not a journal entry. Then move on.

**Final reminder**

Pushback is uncomfortable, but it's not a signal that you must fix the other person's feelings.

If your message was clear and respectful, you can let it stand.

Warmth can stay. Self-blame does not need to return.

**Quick check before you hit send**

Ask:

- Did I add new reasons that invite debate?
- Did I keep the boundary sentence stable?
- Did I choose one repeat line?
- Did I stop?

If yes, you're done.

**Closing line**

You can be kind and still be clear, even when someone pushes back.

# CHAPTER 8
# THE 14-DAY APOLOGY RESET PLAN

You don't change an apology habit by understanding it once.

You change it by practicing the right moves often enough that they become available when you're stressed.

Over-apologizing usually feels automatic in the moment, but it changes the same way other habits change: through small, repeated reps in real situations. Not perfect reps. Not dramatic reps. Just consistent ones.

This chapter turns what you've learned so far into a simple practice plan, so you're not left with good ideas and no clear way to use them.

You now have a set of tools:

- you can spot reflex apologies and separate them from real repair
- you can map triggers and name what "sorry" is trying to prevent
- you can communicate cleanly with one sentence first
- you can choose ladder moves instead of apology padding
- you can apologize well when you are actually wrong
- you can set boundaries without sorry
- you can handle pushback without backtracking

Now we turn those tools into a simple plan you can follow without making your life complicated.

**Start here**

- The goal is accurate apologies, not zero apologies.
- One small rep per day changes your baseline faster than big efforts.
- Each day focuses on one skill and one script category.
- You track progress with receipts, not other people's reactions.
- At the end you'll have a personal script set you can keep using.

**What's really going on**

Over-apologizing is a habit loop.

**Trigger:** tension, uncertainty, timing, a request, a boundary, a shift in someone's mood.

**Reflex:** apologize to smooth and prevent a reaction.

**After-effect:** over-explain, replay the moment, send follow-up apologies.

**Reinforcement:** you feel temporary relief, so the habit strengthens.

This reset plan breaks the loop in three places:

1) awareness, so the reflex is no longer invisible
2) replacement, so you have language other than sorry
3) follow-through, so you don't undo yourself after you speak

You're not trying to become fearless. You're training accuracy and self-trust through small reps.

**Easy mistakes to watch for**

- Trying to do the plan perfectly.
- Measuring success by confidence.
- Choosing the hardest person first.
- Turning the plan into self-criticism.
- Doing too much and burning out.

If you miss a day, you don't restart your life. You continue where you left off.

**How to do this**

**The daily rhythm (10 minutes)**

1) **Pick your one rep**
Choose one likely trigger today.

2) **Choose your move**
Use the ladder move that fits, or the repair apology when needed.

3) **Use one sentence first**
Clarity first. Warmth optional. Self-blame removed.

4) **Hold after speaking**
No follow-up apology. No extra explanation unless it helps logistics.

5) **Log one receipt**
One sentence proof you practiced.

Two questions you use every day

- Am I actually at fault?
- What am I trying to prevent?

Those two questions keep you out of autopilot.

### What this looks like in real life

You're replying later than you wanted.

Your reflex is: *"Sorry for the late reply."*

Run the rhythm:

- trigger: time
- move: appreciation
- one sentence: *"Thanks for your patience. Here's the update."*
- hold: send it, stop
- receipt: *"I used thanks instead of sorry in a late reply."*

That is one rep. One rep changes your baseline.

### The 14-day plan

Use this plan as written. If a day doesn't fit your life, swap it with a day that does. The point is repetition, not perfection.

### How this 14-day reset is organized

Week 1 builds your *Awareness Layer*. You'll practice spotting the reflex and swapping in simple, clean replacements in low-stakes moments.

Week 2 builds your *Response Layer*. You'll practice staying steady when the moment has more pressure, so your new language holds up when it counts.

## WEEK 1

**DAY 1:**
**Awareness without fixing**
Do a sorry tally today. Don't change anything yet. Just notice where it shows up and what you were trying to prevent.

**DAY 2:**
**Remove filler sorry**
Catch one filler sorry and remove it. Use *"quick question"* or a direct opener instead.

**DAY 3:**
**Appreciation for timing**
Replace one timing apology with appreciation:
*"Thanks for your patience"* or *"Thanks for waiting."*

**DAY 4:**
**Clarity instead of apology**
Use "to clarify" once today instead of sorry.

**DAY 5:**
**Ask without apology padding**
Make one request today without *"sorry to bother you."*

**DAY 6:**
**One clean no**
Say no once with a neutral sentence. No story.

**DAY 7:**
**Repair day**
If you made a real mistake, use a clean repair apology.
If not, practice with a small past example.

**WEEK 2**
The goal this week is steadiness when old triggers hit.

**DAY 8:**
**Stop apologizing for feelings**
Notice apologies for emotions. Replace with ownership:
*"I'm feeling overwhelmed, so I'm going to slow down."*

**DAY 9:**
**Stop apologizing for needs**
State one need plainly: *"I need more time,"*
*"I need quiet tonight,"* or *"I need help."*

**DAY 10:**
**Stop apologizing for taking up space**
Catch apology padding when you speak.
Replace with a clear starter: *"I have a question."*

**DAY 11:**
**Practice the broken record**
Repeat a boundary once without adding new reasons.

**DAY 12:**
**Practice exiting a loop**
Use a pause or exit line in a circular conversation.

**DAY 13:**
**One slightly hard rep**
Pick 1 safe uncomfortable moment and use a clean sentence.

**DAY 14:**
**Lock it in**
Review your receipts and choose your top scripts for the next month.

**Practice targets for your reset**

This section helps you keep the plan realistic.

Your goal is not to have zero apologies. Your goal is to reduce unnecessary ones and improve repair.

A reasonable starting point:

- one rep per day
- two boundaries per week
- one repair apology per week if needed

That is enough to create change without making your life about communication practice.

**Scripts you can use**

These script sets are unique to Chapter 8 and focus on the reset plan language.

**Micro script set 1: Daily starter lines**

1) *"Quick question."*
2) *"Thanks for your patience."*
3) *"To clarify, ____."*
4) *"I need more time. I'll reply by ____."*
5) *"Can you ____ by ____?"*
6) *"That won't work for me."*
7) *"My answer is still no."*
8) *"I'm going to pause this conversation."*

**Micro script set 2: Receipt lines to track progress**

1) *"I paused instead of apologizing."*
2) *"I used appreciation instead of sorry."*
3) *"I asked directly and stopped."*
4) *"I clarified once and let it stand."*
5) *"I said no without a story."*
6) *"I repaired without self-attack."*
7) *"I held my boundary with repetition."*
8) *"I exited a loop without guilt."*

**A quick practice**
**Practice: One rep today**

Pick one day from the plan and do one rep today. Then write one receipt sentence.

Small and done is better than big and abandoned.

**Try this**

**Build your 30-day maintenance plan**

The 14-day reset is the start. Maintenance keeps it.

**Step 1: Choose a frequency**
Option A: one rep per day
Option B: three reps per week
Option C: one rep per conversation in one relationship

**Step 2: Choose your top five scripts**
Pick one from each category: appreciation, clarity, request, boundary, pushback.

**Step 3: Choose your trigger card**
Write your top two triggers and your starter line for each.

**Step 4: Schedule your reps**
Put them on your calendar if that helps.

**Step 5: Review weekly**
Once a week, read your receipts and adjust your scripts.

**If this feels hard**

**"I missed a day."**
Continue. Do not restart. The plan is practice, not perfection.

**"I feel awkward using new language."**
Awkward is normal. Keep the rep small.

**"People notice and comment."**
Keep it simple: *"I'm practicing being clearer."*

**"I still apologize sometimes."**
You will. Your goal is accuracy, not zero.

**Take this with you**

- The reset plan changes habits through small reps, not motivation.
- Use the daily rhythm: rep, move, one sentence, hold, receipt.
- Track progress with receipts, not other people's reactions.
- Choose a maintenance plan so the habit sticks.
- Clarity and warmth can coexist without self-blame.

## The plan in a table you can screenshot

If you want this to be easy to use, keep it visible. Here is the plan in a compact format.

| | |
|---|---|
| **Day 1:** | Notice your sorry moments. Label the trigger and what you were trying to prevent. |
| **Day 2:** | Remove one filler sorry. Replace with a direct opener. |
| **Day 3:** | Use appreciation once for timing. |
| **Day 4:** | Use clarity once instead of apology padding. |
| **Day 5:** | Make one clean request. |
| **Day 6:** | Set one small boundary. |
| **Day 7:** | Use the four-part repair if needed. |
| **Day 8:** | Replace "sorry for feeling" with ownership. |
| **Day 9:** | State one need plainly. |
| **Day 10:** | Speak without apology padding once. |
| **Day 11:** | Use the broken record once. |
| **Day 12:** | Exit a loop once. |
| **Day 13:** | Do one slightly hard rep. |
| **Day 14:** | Review receipts and choose top scripts. |

## How to choose your daily rep in 30 seconds

Some days you won't know what to practice. Use this quick method.

1) Look at your day's likely moments:

- messages you need to send
- plans that might shift
- people who tend to trigger you

2) Pick the smallest rep that still counts:

- remove filler
- appreciation for timing
- one clean request
- one clean no
- one clarity statement

3) Write your one sentence before the moment happens.

Pre-writing is how you avoid panic language.

**Extra examples: Receipts that prove progress**

Receipts are simple proof that you practiced. Here are examples you can copy.

- *"I replied late without apologizing and nothing blew up."*
- *"I said no once and didn't write a second message."*
- *"I asked a question without permission language."*
- *"I used a repeat line instead of explaining."*
- *"I apologized once for a real mistake and offered repair."*

These short notes teach your brain that clarity is survivable.

**A simple way to handle days with real stress**

On days where you're exhausted, your goal isn't growth. Your goal isn't slipping into apology spirals.

Use the minimum viable rep:

- one pause line
- one clean sentence
- stop

Example: *"I need more time. I'll reply tomorrow afternoon."*

That is a win on a hard day.

**The "don't undo yourself" rule**

Many people can use clean language once. The habit returns in the follow-up message.

For the next 14 days, use this rule:

If your message was clear and respectful, do not send a second message for ten minutes.

If you feel urgent, write the follow-up in your notes, not in the chat.

After ten minutes, ask: Does this help logistics, or am I trying to prevent a feeling?

If it's about feelings, don't send it.

This one rule prevents a large percentage of apology spirals.

**Day by day guide with one simple prompt**

If you want the plan to feel easier, use one prompt per day. It keeps the rep small.

**Day 1: Awareness**
Prompt: "Where did sorry show up today, and what was I trying to prevent?"
Action: track your sorry moments and label the trigger.

**Day 2: Remove filler**
Prompt: "Where am I using sorry as punctuation?"
Action: remove one filler sorry and send it anyway.

**Day 3: Appreciation for timing**
Prompt: "Where can I replace sorry with thanks?"
Action: use "Thanks for your patience" once.

**Day 4: Clarity**
Prompt: "What do I actually mean?"
Action: use one clarity line: "To clarify, ____."

**Day 5: Requests**
Prompt: "What am I asking for, exactly?"
Action: make one request in one sentence.

**Day 6: One clean no**
Prompt: "What limit do I need today?"
Action: say no once without a story.

**Day 7: Repair practice**
Prompt: "Did I cause harm or break an agreement?"
Action: use the four-part apology once if needed, or write it as practice.

**Day 8: Feelings without apology**
Prompt: "What feeling am I apologizing for?"
Action: replace it with ownership: "I'm feeling ____ and I'm going to ____."

**Day 9: Needs without apology**
Prompt: "What do I need right now?"
Action: state one need plainly.

**Day 10: Space without apology**
Prompt: "Where am I shrinking to be liked?"
Action: speak once without apology padding.

**Day 11: Broken record**
Prompt: "Can I repeat my boundary without new reasons?"
Action: repeat once and stop.

**Day 12: Exit**
Prompt: "Is this conversation turning circular?"
Action: use one pause or exit line.

**Day 13: Slightly hard rep**
Prompt: "What would be a brave but safe sentence today?"
Action: do one rep with a higher trigger person.

**Day 14: Lock in**
Prompt: "What worked, and what do I want to keep?"
Action: choose your top five scripts and your maintenance plan.

## The three script packs you'll use most

To make the plan usable, you need a small set of scripts you can reach for quickly. These packs are meant to be copied into your notes.

### Pack 1: Timing and updates

- *"Thanks for your patience. Here's the update."*
- *"Thanks for waiting. I'll be there at ____."*
- *"I need more time. I'll reply by ____."*
- *"I'm running late. I'll arrive at ____."*
- *"I can't respond fully right now. I'll reply by ____."*
- *"I saw this. I'll get back to you by ____."*
- *"I'm available after ____, not before."*
- *"I need to reschedule. Can we do ____ instead?"*

### Pack 2: Requests and clarity

- *"Quick question: ____."*
- *"Can you send ____ by ____?"*
- *"Can you help me with ____?"*
- *"To clarify, I mean ____."*
- *"Let me restate what I mean: ____."*
- *"Which option do you prefer?"*
- *"What time are we aiming for?"*
- *"I want to be accurate, so let me check."*

**Pack 3: Boundaries and pushback**

- *"That won't work for me."*
- *"I can't do that."*
- *"My answer is still no."*
- *"I hear you. I still can't."*
- *"I'm going to pause this conversation."*
- *"We can talk later when we're calmer."*
- *"I'm not discussing that."*
- *"I'm going to end this call now."*

These packs work because they are plain. Plain language is easier to use under stress.

**How to handle mistakes during the reset**

You will still apologize unnecessarily sometimes. That's not failure. It's data. When you catch it, do a quick reset instead of self-criticism.

1) Name it: "That was a reflex apology."
2) Name the job: "I was trying to prevent ____."
3) Choose the swap: appreciation, clarity, request, boundary.
4) Practice once next time.

If you want to correct a message you already sent, keep it short. Instead of a long follow-up apology, use a clean restatement:

- *"Let me restate that clearly: ____." OR*
- *"Thanks for your patience. Here's what I mean: ____."*

This keeps you out of a spiral.

**How to choose your top five scripts on Day 14**

Your top scripts should be the ones you will actually use, not the ones that sound impressive.

Choose scripts that:

- match your most common triggers
- are short enough to remember
- feel natural in your voice
- reduce your urge to over-explain

A balanced top five includes:

- one appreciation line
- one clarity line
- one request line
- one boundary line
- one pushback line

Example set:

*"Thanks for your patience."*
*"To clarify, ____."*
*"Can you ____ by ____?"*
*"That won't work for me."*
*"My answer is still no."*

**Maintenance plan options**

After the 14 days, you don't need more content. You need repetition.

*Pick one:*
**Option A:** one rep per day
**Option B:** three reps per week
**Option C:** one rep per conversation in one relationship

The best plan is the one you will actually do when you are busy.

**Try this: The 14-day receipt sheet**

This exercise turns your plan into something you can complete.

**Step 1:** Create a simple list with Day 1 to Day 14.
**Step 2:** Next to each day, write the focus word.
**Step 3:** Each day, write one receipt sentence only.
**Step 4:** If you miss a day, leave it blank and keep going.
**Step 5:** On Day 14, read all receipts and circle the three that felt most empowering.
**Step 6:** Turn those three into your "keep" scripts.

Receipt sentence examples:

- "I used thanks instead of sorry."
- "I asked directly and stopped."
- "I said no without a story."
- "I repeated my boundary once."
- "I apologized once and offered repair."

The receipt sheet is valuable because it creates proof. Proof builds self-trust.

**Scenario add-on: The day you get a strong reaction**

Sometimes you'll do a rep and the other person will react poorly. That can make you want to give up.

Use this response plan:

1) Pause one breath.
2) Reflect: "I hear you."
3) Repeat your sentence.
4) Exit if the conversation becomes disrespectful.

Then write the receipt anyway:
"I stayed clear even with discomfort."

You're training your nervous system to tolerate normal tension.

**A simple schedule that fits real life**

If "one rep per day" feels vague, attach it to something you already do.

Choose one anchor:

- after breakfast
- after lunch
- after dinner
- before bed
- after you send your first message of the day

Then do the smallest rep:

- remove one filler sorry
- send one clean request
- use one appreciation line
- use one clarity line
- set one small boundary

Anchors reduce decision fatigue.

**What to do if you feel yourself slipping back**

Old habits return under stress. That's normal.

When you notice yourself apologizing excessively again, don't restart the whole plan. Do a three-day reset:

Day 1: appreciation for timing once
Day 2: one clean request
Day 3: one clean boundary

Three days is enough to restore your baseline.

**Final reminder**

The plan works when you keep the rep small and consistent. You're not trying to impress anyone. You're building a new default.

**The "if then" plan for your top triggers**

If you want speed, write an "if then" plan for the two triggers that show up most.

"If then" plans are powerful because they remove thinking from the moment.

Examples:

- If I'm replying late, then I will use appreciation: *"Thanks for your patience. Here's the update."*
- If someone's tone shifts, then I will gather info: *"Is now a good time to talk?"*
- If I need to say no, then I will use a neutral boundary: *"That won't work for me."*
- If I need to clarify, then I will use a clarity line: *"To clarify, ____."*

Write your two most common "if then" plans in your notes and use them for the full 14 days. This creates repetition where it matters most.

**The two-minute rule for follow-up messages**

If your old pattern is sending a second apology, use this rule: Wait two minutes before sending any follow-up.

During those two minutes, ask:

- Is this follow-up about logistics?
- Or is it about preventing a feeling?

If it's about logistics, keep it to one sentence. If it's about preventing a feeling, don't send it. This rule protects your progress more than almost anything else.

## A final script set you can keep

Here are eight "default sentences" that cover most daily moments. They are normal. They are calm. They work.

1) *"Quick question."*
2) *"Thanks for your patience."*
3) *"To clarify, ____."*
4) *"I need more time. I'll reply by ____."*
5) *"Can you ____ by ____?"*
6) *"That won't work for me."*
7) *"My answer is still no."*
8) *"I'm going to pause this conversation."*

If you only remember two, make them:
*"Thanks for your patience,"* and *"That won't work for me."*

## Closing encouragement that stays practical

If you've spent years smoothing, clarity will feel unfamiliar at first. That does not mean it's wrong.

This plan is not about being perfect. It's about building a small set of behaviors you can repeat when you're tired, stressed, or unsure.

Keep the reps small. Keep the language plain. Let your messages stand. That's how the habit changes.

## Final note

On Day 14, choose your top five scripts and keep using them. That's the real reset. Keep it simple. Always.

# PRINTABLE
# THE APOLOGY HABIT RESET 14-DAY STEP GUIDE

**How to use this guide**

Do one rep per day. Keep it small. If you miss a day, continue with the next day rather than restarting. Your goal is accurate apologies, not zero apologies.

**Daily rhythm (10 minutes)**

1) Pick one likely trigger today.

2) Choose your move: remove filler, appreciation, clarity, request, boundary, or repair (only if you're actually wrong).

3) Use one sentence first. Warmth is optional. Self-blame is not required.

4) Hold after speaking: no follow-up apology or extra explanation unless it helps logistics.

5) Log one receipt sentence (proof you practiced).

**Two questions to ask daily**

- Am I actually at fault?
- What am I trying to prevent?

## The 14-day plan

### Day 1: Awareness

Action: Do a sorry tally. Don't change anything yet. Label the trigger type and what you were trying to prevent.

Receipt: "I noticed my sorry hot spots today."

### Day 2: Remove filler

Action: Remove one filler sorry (punctuation sorry). Replace with a direct opener like "Quick question."

Receipt: "I removed filler sorry once."

### Day 3: Appreciation for timing

Action: Replace one timing apology with appreciation: "Thanks for your patience" or "Thanks for waiting."

Receipt: "I used thanks instead of sorry for timing."

### Day 4: Clarity

Action: Use one clarity line instead of apology padding: "To clarify, ____."

Receipt: "I clarified once and let it stand."

### Day 5: Requests

Action: Make one request without apology padding. Keep it one sentence.

Receipt: "I asked directly and stopped."

### Day 6: One clean no

Action: Say no once with a neutral sentence. No story.

Receipt: "I said no without a story."

**Day 7: Repair day**

Action: If you made a real mistake, use a clean repair apology. If not, write a practice apology for a small past moment.

Receipt: "I repaired without self-attack."

**Day 8: Feelings without apology**

Action: Notice one apology for a feeling. Replace with ownership: "I'm feeling ___ and I'm going to ___."

Receipt: "I owned a feeling without apologizing for it."

**Day 9: Needs without apology**

Action: State one need plainly: time, space, help, quiet, or clarity.

Receipt: "I stated a need plainly."

**Day 10: Space without apology**

Action: Speak once without apology padding. Start with: "I have a question" or "I want to be clear."

Receipt: "I spoke without shrinking."

**Day 11: Broken record**

Action: Repeat a boundary once without adding new reasons.

Receipt: "I repeated my boundary once."

**Day 12: Exit a loop**

Action: Use a pause or exit line in a circular or tense conversation: "I'm going to pause this."

Receipt: "I paused a loop without guilt."

**Day 13: Slightly hard rep**

Action: Choose one uncomfortable but safe moment and use a clean sentence. Keep it short.

Receipt: "I stayed clear in a harder moment."

**Day 14: Lock it in**

Action: Review all receipts. Choose your top five scripts for the next month and your maintenance plan.

Receipt: "I chose my top five scripts."

Top five scripts (fill in): Choose one from each category

- Appreciation: ______________________________
- Clarity: ______________________________
- Request: ______________________________
- Boundary: ______________________________
- Pushback: ______________________________

**30-day maintenance** (choose one)

Option A: One rep per day
Option B: Three reps per week
Option C: One rep per conversation in one relationship

My plan: ______________________________

**Simple rule that prevents apology spirals**

If your message was clear and respectful, don't send a second message for 10 minutes. If you still want to send something, keep it to one sentence that helps logistics.

# CONCLUSION

If you've made it to the end of this book, you already have something useful: a repeatable way to respond when the urge to apologize shows up.

That matters more than getting every conversation right.

The goal was never to remove the word sorry from your life. The goal was to stop using it as a reflex that makes you smaller, less clear, or less honest than you need to be.

You now have a practical system you can return to.

You know how to pause long enough to ask whether you're actually at fault, and what you're trying to prevent. You know how to separate real repair from reflex smoothing. You know how to use cleaner language when you need to clarify, ask, set a boundary, or hold your ground. You also know how to apologize properly when you are wrong, without turning repair into self-punishment.

That's real progress.

It may not feel dramatic. It may not look dramatic from the outside. But in everyday life, this kind of change adds up quickly.

- A cleaner sentence instead of an apology spiral.
- A boundary that stays in place.
- A request that doesn't come wrapped in self-blame.
- A moment of pushback that doesn't pull you back into over-explaining.

Those aren't small things. They change how you move through conversations, and they change how you feel afterward.

**Accuracy over perfection**

If you remember only one idea from this book, let it be this: Accuracy is a better goal than perfection.

You don't need to become a flawless communicator. You don't need to sound polished in every moment. You don't need to stop caring what people think.

- You only need to become more accurate.
- Apologize when you caused harm or broke an agreement.
- Use a better tool when you're not at fault.
- Keep warmth through respect, not self-blame.
- Let a clear message stand.

That's enough to build a new baseline.

**When you slip**

You'll still over-apologize sometimes. That doesn't mean the reset failed. It means you're human, and habits come back under stress.

What matters is what you do next. When you notice it, keep the response simple:

- Name it: "That was a reflex apology."
- Name the job: "I was trying to prevent ____."
- Choose the better move for next time.

Then move on.

You don't need a long postmortem. You don't need to punish yourself. You don't need to restart from zero.

You need your next rep.

**How to keep this going without making it a project**

You already built your foundation in Chapter 8. You don't need more content right now. You need repetition.

- Keep it light.
- Keep it realistic.
- Keep using the tools in ordinary moments.

- A late reply.
- A small request.
- A simple no.
- A clarification.
- A moment of pressure where you choose a pause instead of a panic apology.

That's where this work becomes a habit.

If you stop and start, that's fine. If you do well for a week and then have a messy day, that's fine. If some relationships shift as you become clearer, that's normal.

You're not doing this to become harder.

You're doing it so your kindness is no longer paid for with self-blame.

## A better way to measure progress

Try not to measure your progress by whether everyone responds well.

Some people will appreciate your clarity right away. Some will need time. Some may never like that your language has changed.

Their reaction is information, but it's not your scoreboard.

*A better measure is this:*

Are you becoming more honest, more accurate, and steadier in the moments that used to pull you into automatic sorry?

If the answer is yes, even sometimes, the habit is changing.

## Final reminder

You can be warm and clear at the same time.

You can apologize when it matters and stop apologizing when it does not.

You can care about the relationship without taking blame for everything that happens inside it.

- Keep your language simple.
- Keep your expectations realistic.
- Keep practicing.

That's how the apology habit changes.
One clean rep at a time.

# ACKNOWLEDGMENTS

Thank you to every reader who's ever swallowed a boundary, softened a need, or apologized for taking up space, then wondered why they felt drained afterward.

This book exists because so many people are kind, thoughtful, and careful, and still end up carrying responsibility that isn't theirs.

Thank you to the friends, clients, and everyday conversations that revealed the pattern over and over again: the apology that repairs is powerful, but the apology that prevents discomfort can quietly shrink a person over time. Seeing that clearly shaped every page.

Thank you to the readers who want practical tools more than big speeches. Your preference for calm language, usable scripts, and real-life practice is what guided this book's approach.

And finally, thank you to anyone learning to be clearer while still being warm. That combination is not only possible. It's often the most respectful way to communicate. You're allowed to be kind without self-blame, and you're allowed to practice it one small rep at a time.

# About the Author

Amelia Oliver-Lilly writes calm, practical nonfiction for people who want clearer communication and steadier self-trust without turning life into a self-improvement project. Her work focuses on simple frameworks, clean language, and small, repeatable habits that make everyday moments easier to handle.

She's especially drawn to the quiet patterns that keep good people stuck, like over-apologizing, over-explaining, and shrinking to keep the peace. Rather than pushing readers toward harsh "confidence" tactics, Amelia offers grounded tools that keep warmth intact while removing unnecessary self-blame.

*The Apology Habit Reset* is built for real life. It's script-first, non-preachy, and designed for practice in low-stakes moments, so the skills show up when it counts. If you like books that are respectful, clear, and immediately usable, you're in the right place.

www.ingramcontent.com/pod-product-compliance
Lightning Source LLC
Chambersburg PA
CBHW052354060726
47592CB00020B/2243